Irresistible Influence

You Can Also Make a Difference

Gregory Lan Ijiwola

CityLight
Publications

Chicago, IL

All scripture quotations, unless otherwise indicated, are taken from the New King James Version®. Copyright © 1982 by Thomas Nelson, Inc. Used by permission. All rights reserved. Scripture quotations marked (AMP) are taken from the Amplified Bible, Copyright © 1954, 1958, 1962, 1964, 1965, 1987 by The Lockman Foundation. Used by permission. Scriptures marked (MSG) are taken from The Message. Copyright © 1993, 1994, 1995, 1996, 2000, 2001, 2002. Used by permission of NavPress Publishing Group. The author may emphasize some Scripture quotations in bold type.

Irresistible Influence
You Can Also Make a Difference

ISBN: 0-9746735-3-6
ISBN 13: 978-0-9746735-3-0
Copyright © 2011 by Gregory Lan Ijiwola

Published by
CityLight Publications
P.O Box 15478
Chicago, IL 60615
www.thecitylight.org

Cover design by GodKulture, LLC.

Printed in the United States of America. All rights reserved under International Copyright Law. No part of this publication may be reproduced, stored in a retrieval system or be transmitted in any form or by any means, mechanical, electronic, photocopying or otherwise without the express written consent of the publisher except by a reviewer who may quote brief passages in a review.

CONTENTS

Dedication iv

Acknowledgements v

Introduction... vii

Chapter 1: What is Influence? 1

Chapter 2: The Necessity of an Influential Life 13

Chapter 3: Under the Influence......................... 27

Chapter 4: Associating With Influence 43

Chapter 5: Influential Prayer 59

Chapter 6: What's Your Thing?......................... 79

Chapter 7: The Salt Factor................................99

Chapter 8: Leading Influence............................118

Chapter 9: Money and Influence......................129

Chapter 10: Let Your Light Shine......................149

DEDICATION

To Pastor Sunday Adelaja, who has taught me how to live a life of influence by precepts and example. Your teachings at the History Makers Training spurred me into writing again after several years of hiatus. You awakened a sleeping giant within me.

To Debo, my partner in life. Thanks for your commitment and dedication. Your life continues to influence me more than that of any human.

ACKNOWLEDGEMENTS

Writing a book is a team effort. I appreciate everyone who contributed in any way to make this book a reality. Special thanks to all the members of the CityLight Church. Working together with you to spread the light of God in Chicago spurred me to embark on writing this book and shaped my ideas of the concepts of living a relevant and influential life. Many thanks to Ranti Ihimoyan and Emi Aprekuma for giving form to my rudimentary ideas through their tireless editorial efforts.

Unending thanks to my wife, Debo, for being the finisher that you are; spending numerous hours in sharpening my ideas and typesetting the manuscript. And I'm ever thankful to my children: Jesse, Joshua and Pearl, who lovingly and graciously allowed "Daddy" to have uninterrupted time to focus on writing.

Introduction

There are two tools you use often, albeit, sometimes unknowingly, that perfectly illustrate the subject of this book. I would like to start with them. One is the thermometer and the other is the thermostat.

Every time you check the temperature of your house, glance at the temperature display in your car or check your body temperature, you are utilizing the service of a thermometer. It is an instrument that measures temperature. There are many types of thermometers, but they all function by the same principle, the ability of the environment to affect some characteristics of the thermometer in proportion to the rise or fall in temperature. The thermometer functions by being affected. It responds to changes in the environment but does nothing to affect the environment.

The thermostat, on the other hand, is a different instrument. It functions in the opposite way a thermometer functions. Instead of responding to changes in the environment, it dictates it. Whenever you want to change the temperature of your house or car, it is the thermostat you use. The thermostat is an influence. The thermometer is not. The thermostat tells the environment how to behave; the thermometer behaves as dictated by the environment.

This book is about influence. It is about becoming a thermostat in your world. It is about you no longer living your life responding to the stimuli of your environment, submitting to its dictate. It is about using your God-given abilities and opportunities to create change and to leave a legacy in the world. It is about fulfilling God's dream for your life and helping many others along the way. It is aimed at turning you from

Introduction

responder to influencer; from reactive to proactive; from a spectator to a successful actor.

You have a destiny to fulfill that requires the ability to move things in your favor. It requires the cooperation of people and the garnering of resources. The goal is to enhance your ability to lead, persuade, motivate and release favor in order to touch your world in a significant way for the glory of God.

I assume you want to be a person of influence. Picking up this book seems to suggest so. You want to hit the target God shot you into this world as an arrow to hit. You want your life to be significant for God. It is not your desire to remain as one of those who pass through life without a making mark, living mediocre lives.

Also, we prayed over this book before it was released. We prayed that it will only get into the hands of those who desperately need it: those whose hearts are panting for the content of its pages. Some will know they need it in their intellects. For others it will be the pull from the hunger of their hearts that draws it to them.

So no matter how it got into your hand, there is something in it for you. In the following pages, I will share some truth with you from scriptures that will expand your mind and lift you to new heights in your ability to impact your world. We will examine principles of influence that have worked for the greatest influencers that have walked our world and have added much good to it. We will study the greatest influencer of all, the Lord Jesus Christ, and learn from His life.

Read it in a quiet place where you can reflect without distractions. As you read, pray for God to open your eyes to see His intention in your life to be an influence for Him and His kingdom in the spheres that He has put you. Ask Him to show you how to go about exerting this influence. Then practice what you learn from the book. If the truths espoused impacts your life, pass the book along and share it with others. Write me a

Introduction

note if you choose to and let me know the good it did in your life. I'll be glad to hear from you.

CHAPTER 1

What is Influence?

"Influence may be the highest level of human skills" – Author Unknown

Before we delve deep into the subject of influence, it is important to know what it is and what it is not. Merriam-Webster's dictionary defines influence as "the power or capacity to cause an effect in indirect or intangible ways."[1] It is the ability to affect things and people, motivating and causing them to act in certain ways. Influence is the ability to sway—the power to cause people to follow.

Various entities wield influence. For example, entities like MTV have enormous influence over the younger generation. The fast food industry is another entity that wields enormous influence over youth. Whenever my kids and I are out driving, they never fail to notice the golden arches of the McDonald logo. The arches always elicit the same response; my children instantly become hungry and the only food that can satisfy their hunger is a happy meal!

Media organizations also exert tremendous influence. They dictate trends and cause people to adopt certain views, behaviors and expectations.

People are some of the greatest sources of influence. From celebrities who dictate manners of language and dressing to followers and politicians who move massive crowds of people, to mothers who mold the life of their children by the example they show.

Think of people like Billy Graham, Mother Theresa, Barack Obama, Steve Jobs, Rick Warren, Bill Gates, Martin Luther-King Jr., Enoch Adeboye, Bill Bright, Michael Jackson, Beyoncé, Angelina Jolie, Oprah etc. All these people have something in common.

What is Influence?

They all have exhibited the power to move people and things in a particular direction, without force, coercion or direct exertion. They are trendsetters. They inspire followers.

Jesus Christ stands out arguably as the most influential man of all time. Though He lived an earthly life of only 33 years, the world has yet to recover from His influence. In His time, no one was indifferent to Him; Jesus elicited intense responses from all who came in contact with Him.

On the one hand, the established religious authorities of Christ's time reviled him and went to great extents to see him expelled from their towns. Ultimately, this establishment pressed for His arrest and brutal crucifixion.

Other people, however, went as far as relinquishing all their possessions to follow Him. Large crowds of people sought His audience. Multitudes traveled long distances just to hear him speak. The rich, the poor, nobles and commoners alike transformed their lives in order to follow His teaching and example. Jesus had irresistible influence.

Even after His earthly life, Jesus' influence is still pervasive. His principles have influenced most of our social infrastructure. For example, Jesus' followers spread teachings that helped eradicate many common savage practices of the time such as human sacrifice, mutilation and cannibalism.

Jesus' followers took an active role in revolutionizing our educational and governmental systems. Christianity's influence can be seen in the numerous educational systems around the world founded and maintained by Christians.

In fact, Harvard University, one of the most esteemed American universities' initial motto was *Veritas Christo et Ecclesiae*—"Truth for Christ and the Church". In addition to maintaining reputable schools, Christian organizations have established and run a great

What is Influence?

percentage of the world's hospitals, orphanages, relief organizations and charities.

Christian influence has also been felt in the sciences, arts, and architecture. Christian practitioners in these fields, such as the geneticist Gregor Mendel and renowned artist and architect Michelangelo's accomplishments are as widely celebrated as those of their non-Christian counterparts.

Jesus' influence has even been felt in literature. In addition to the Bible, numerous literary works deemed classics, from Dante's *Inferno* to John Milton's *Paradise Lost*, have consistently been regarded as standards in literature.

Finally, Jesus' philosophies established an ideal for justice, compassion and mercy—elevating women's social standing in society, driving the abolition of slavery, and leading efforts aimed at garnering society's respect for the dignity and rights of all humans, born and unborn.

In fact, two influential civil rights leaders of the 20th century, Gandhi and Martin Luther King Jr., credit Jesus' teachings for inspiring their efforts to get their respective governments to protect the rights of their people. Jesus' influence, centuries after his death, cannot be overstated.

The examples of influence I have given range from that of MTV to that of Christ. This range demonstrates that influence is a neutral tool. Influence is simply the power to motivate and persuade.

However, just as you could use your knife to cut your sandwich in two in order to share it with another person, you could also use that same knife to cut and hurt the person. Thus, the knife is neutral in that it does not carry an intrinsic goodness or evil. Rather, its goodness is created by how it is used.

Though some people cringe at the subject of influence because it dredges up negative connotations in their minds, a similar logic applies to influence. That is,

What is Influence?

much like the knife in the example, influence does not have an internal negative or positive. However, by endeavoring to be an irresistible influence like Christ, you are attempting to harness the positive power of influence. This positive influence is the subject matter of this book.

Some concepts such as manipulation, coercion, popularity, and position sometimes masquerade as influence, but they lack the transforming power of influence. They are not the tools of one who seeks to be an irresistible influence.

What Influence is Not

1. Manipulation

Manipulation is the devious use of power to sway the actions of others for the actor's own advantage, usually at the other person's expense. Manipulation is selfish, evil and not of God. Many powerful leaders have resorted to manipulation, taking advantage of unsuspecting followers to enrich themselves.

For example, some preachers and tele-evangelist have used their power to swindle people of money. Some cult leaders have notoriously used their skills to cause followers to become wholly submissive to them (the cult leaders). At times these cult leaders' control run so deep that they are able to convince the cult members to take their own lives.

Similarly, some parents utilize their power over their children in corrosive ways. Over time, these parents have manipulated their children by supplanting their desires with those of the child, at times even placing their children in marriages and/or careers that fulfill the parent's dreams rather than the child's.

2. Coercion

Coercion is the act of getting cooperation through intimidation, pressure or threats. Though coercion may give you control over others' actions, it is not influence.

What is Influence?

I sometimes resort to coercion. If you are a parent, you probably know about the vegetable stand-off. Though most children know vegetables are good for them, they often refuse to eat them.

When my kids make their stance against vegetables, I usually respond with gentle persuasions. As my children maintain their refusal, I usually resort to more and more coercive methods. A staple of mine is the age old, "Eat your vegetables, or else."

This method often works with my children, but with lots of tears and crying accompanying dinner time. It is obvious that this is not influence. Influence empowers and motivates; coercion forces.

3. Popularity

Popularity is how appealing, favored or admired you are by the general public. Though popularity can give you influence, it is not influence. These days, influence and clout is often rated by fame, the number of

Facebook friends or Twitter "followers", your reach, and name recognition.

However, these are not true measures of influence. Reach is not synonymous with influence. You can have thousands of "friends" and "followers" without creating any meaningful influence. Influence goes beyond simply knowing and reaching people or amassing "friends".

4. Position

Position is where you are placed in life. Titles, roles, and designations all fall under this subcategory. Much like popularity, you can have position without influence. Position often seems like influence because it bestows power. However, position motivates people to follow simply because of the position's place in society, not because of the person's individual ability to influence.

For example, if a uniformed police officer shouts, "Stop! I'm a police officer." Most people will stop simply

What is Influence?

because society has designated policemen with the authority to stop people. That is, people's response to the officer is not motivated by the individual, but by the position.

Thus, position is not as meaningful as influence because people follow you, not because they *want* to, but because they *have* to.

Our discussion of manipulation, coercion, popularity and position leads to one conclusion: these four are shells of influence. From a distance they seem to be synonymous with influence, but close inspection shows these attributes cannot live up to the dynamic force that is influence.

In the next chapter, I will focus on why you should be a person of irresistible influence.

CHAPTER 2

The Necessity of an Influential Life

"All that is necessary for the triumph of evil is that good men do nothing" – Edmund Burke

I call the first two chapters of Genesis the most "perfect" chapters of the bible. In these chapters, everything was good. Sin had not entered into the world. There was no death or decay. Adam and Eve were in fellowship with God and each other. The devil had not made his debut. These two chapters reveal everything as it was supposed to be. (In fact, the rest of the bible aims at getting things back to the way they were in these two chapters.)

Created for Influence

One of the things we see in Genesis 1 is the creation of man. In verse 26, God speaks to Himself,

> *"And God said, let us make man in our own image and after our likeness and let them have dominion..."*
> *(Genesis 1:26).*

This verse shows that Adam and Eve were created to exert influence over all of God's creation. Adam and Eve were put in the Garden of Eden which was saturated in God's presence and given the assignment of spreading that glory all over the face of the earth.

That is, they were filled with God's glory so that they could exert dominion. A major element of dominion is influence. At their creation, Adam and Eve were fully under the influence of God and were to spread that dominion—in this case, influence—everywhere they went.

This assignment was not only geographical. Adam and Eve's mandate from God was to fill every sphere of the earth with His influence. As the arts developed, they were to express God's glory and beauty through them.

Similarly, as the business field developed, the couple was supposed to fill it with His glory. The same goes for the media, education, family and government spheres. Every sphere of human endeavor was meant to be immersed in God's influence through the influence of humanity. This was the original assignment of humanity.

In the third chapter of Genesis, Satan came in and messed up the plan. He tempted humans to sin. As a result of sin, human beings fell short of God's glory. Instead of being influenced by God, humans came under Satan's influence.

As a result of this change, humans began to spread the influence of Satan. Instead of God's glory, Satan's gloom was spread through creation. The characteristics of Satan began to spread all around the earth.

God's purposes are unchangeable (see Romans 11:29). Despite humanity's satanic deviation, God's purpose for us remains the same. He still expects us to spread His influence and has provided us a means to accomplish this task. We are to exercise dominion over the earth and utilize all its abundant resource to establish the will of God here.

The ability to do this was greatly hindered by the fall of man, through which the control of the earth system was handed over by Adam to Satan thus crowning Satan as the god of this world (See Luke 4:5, 2 Corinthians 4:4).

However, Christ's death and resurrection gave us victory over Satan. Therefore, our authority on earth, which was temporarily lost, has now been restored. By putting our trust in the sacrifice Christ made for us, we once again can claim our dominion and successfully accomplish our assignment (Matthew 28:18-20).

Influence is a Mandate

Another word for "mandate" is "commission". God has given every believer a three-part commission. In order to fulfill these three parts you must grasp your God given influence.

The first part of the commission comes from Matthew 28: 18-19: "And Jesus came and spoke to them, saying, *"All authority has been given to Me in heaven and on earth. Go therefore and make disciples of all the nations..."* Through this verse, Jesus commissions us to influence people and nations to accept Christ and adopt His ways.

The second part of your commission is its sphere. Your sphere consists of your workplace, school, city, church, and community and includes various sectors such as arts and entertainment, business, church, media, educational, family or government sphere. God has placed you in a unique sphere which you are uniquely gifted to influence. He wants you to exercise your dominion over your sphere until people around you come to Christ and the systems within your sphere conform to God's will and bring Him glory as they were originally intended to. You are called to be a culture warrior who strives to influence your sphere with the ways of God.

Your family is the most important section of your God assigned sphere. Through your influence, your spouse and children should be drawn to God. Your family' proximity gives it the ability to be the greatest asset or hindrance in fulfilling your commission.

Therefore, your family must be deeply entrenched in God's influence so that you can stay on track. In order to accomplish this, you must carry out your mandate of surrounding your family in God's influence. This influence must overpower the numerous earthly influences warring for your family's allegiance.

The Necessity Of an Influential Life

The World Needs Good Influence

Life abhors vacuums. Jesus illustrates this idea in Luke 11:24-26. He explains that once an evil spirit has been expelled from a place it will attempt to return. If the evil force finds its former home empty, it brings more evil forces to occupy the territory.

When a place is void of good influence it becomes a haven for evil. If good people stand by and do nothing, then others will fill the vacuum. If there is a void of good influencers, it will be filled by the bad.

In the past, Christians had significant roles in all arenas. However, in the last century, Christians have withdrawn from their leadership role in school systems, politics, media, entertainment, sports, business and other molders of culture.

Christians have focused solely on preparing people for the afterlife. They have overlooked the importance of training Christians to occupy the earth till the Lord returns. Satan has capitalized on this Christian absence.

As a result, many institutions have been turned over to godless purposes. One example is the music industry. Though music is meant to be as a tool of worship and inspiration, it has been perverted by satanic influences. The music industry's most successful artists are usually scantily clad males and females who sing and rap lyrics promoting lust, violence, greed and other forms of licentiousness.

In the music industry, top Christian artists sell a fraction of the number of CDs and concert tickets sold by average secular artists. Christian music has been pushed out of the mainstream and is dribbled out solely by Christian radio stations.

Because Christians have abdicated our commission, Christianity is threatened with irrelevance. Though we are called to influence, we are now subject to the influence of that which should be under our dominion.

The erosion in the music industry can also be seen in private institutions. God-created institutions such as marriage are now governed by secular ideals. The divorce rate and ever growing support for gay marriage show that the world is now defining God's institution.

As a result, the family is no longer under the influence of God. This leads to a greater number of youth who are not being transitioned into adulthood by godly families. Thus, our men and women are increasingly people who cannot carry out the commission to spread God's influence Children and youths are crying out for good role models. The original concept of marriage needs to be redefined by those who still hold to its sacredness.

Everywhere we look; there is a cry for men of integrity and character. This is an opportunity for you. If you ever doubted that God has a specific purpose for you, the shambles in which we find our social systems should motivate you to arise as an irresistible influence.

The Threat of Irrelevance

You are not simply a spot-filler in this world. Influence maintains your relevance. You are not called to just occupy space in the world but to make an impact. Jesus, addressing this says,

"You are the salt of the earth; but if the salt loses its flavor, how shall it be seasoned? It is then good for nothing but to be thrown out and trampled underfoot by men"
(Matthew 5:14).

Salt has been used as a food preservative since ancient times. Meat that has been salted can be preserved for many years. Salt works as a preservative because its presence in food reduces the water content, thus stopping the growth of the bacteria that spoil food. Salt also protects food from mold.

The Necessity Of an Influential Life

Just as the presence of salt preserves food from destruction, the presence of believers in a location should have the same effect. God told Abraham in Genesis 18, that if He could just find ten righteous people in Sodom and Gomorrah, He would spare the land from destruction.

Because there were not even ten righteous people, the land was not saved from destruction. The absence of ten righteous people shows Lot had failed in his role of influence. Not only had he not displayed influence in his broader sphere of these cities, he had not displayed influence in his family. Lot had not even influenced ten people to be obedient to God.

How would biblical history have changed if God had found ten righteous people in Sodom? If at least the whole of Lot's family had been faithful, the two cities may have been preserved.

Sodom and Gomorrah's demise teaches us that, as believers, our presence in our families and communities are strategic. We are meant to add our flavor to the earth, to act as preservatives and make it saltier. We are spaced out and placed into the world in an arrangement that allows us to provide the exact amount of salt our spheres needs.

We are meant to have influence for good over what is going on in our families, cities, and nations. Jesus said if we lose that ability, then our Christianity becomes worthless and useless. Even those we are meant to influence for good, start to step on us in disdain. We become irrelevant.

Our churches are battling irrelevance because we huddle together like salt in salt-shakers, enjoying our relationships with God and one another. We season (and re-season) each other while the saltless communities surrounding us deteriorate. This has had a disastrous effect on younger generations. The Barna Group, in a survey of 22,103 adults and 2, 124 teenagers from January 2001 to through August 2006, found that 61% of

The Necessity Of an Influential Life

today's young adults who had been churched at some point during their teen years become spiritually disengaged (not actively attending church, reading the Bible, or praying) after high school.[2] The majority of these youth remained disengaged in their adult lives. They had a taste of church but it lost its relevance to their lives.

This is happening in the general population as well. Jon Meacham, in a 2009 Time Magazine article, *The End of Christian America*, referred to a survey on American Religious Identification which found that the percentage of self-identified Christians had fallen 10 percentage points since 1990, from 86 to 76 percent.

On the other hand, the number of people who describe themselves as atheist or agnostic had increased about fourfold from 1990 to 2009, from 1 million to about 3.6 million. There is a growing perception that Christianity is judgmental, old-fashioned, hypocritical and irrelevant to the issues confronting people in the

21st century.[3] Though these perceptions may be exaggerated, they still warn of a general trend that Christians must reverse with influence. Your impact in your sphere of influence is an important part of doing this.

In the next chapter, I will begin to share with you some personal strategies to increase your influence in your sphere of life. You will see that the first step to becoming more influential is to be under the right influence yourself.

CHAPTER 3

Under the Influence

"People never improve unless they look to some standard or example higher and better than themselves."
- Tyron Edwards

The earth's two main sources of light, the sun and moon, illustrate the concept of influence. The sun is a primary source of light. It contains more than 99.8% of the total mass of the solar system, making it the largest object in the solar system. Massive nuclear fusion reactions continuously occur within the core of the sun, generating tons of energy which become mostly visible light by the time it reaches the sun's surface. This light then spreads out all around the solar system, enabling life on earth.

IRRESISTIBLE INFLUENCE

The moon is the second brightest object in the sky. However, it is not a primary source of light. That is, the moon has no light of its own. The moonlight that reaches earth is reflected from the sun. The moon, as a result of its perfect positioning in the path of the sun's rays, gets its own glow and floods the night sky with illumination. The relationship between the sun and the moon demonstrates how influence works.

Irresistible influence has a source. It is not self-generated. It comes by positioning yourself under the right influence. In order to influence, you must be influenced yourself. You must constantly be under the influence of God and others aligned with God. The influence under which you position yourself culminates.

It is this culmination of influence on your life that you are meant to spread. The better influenced you are, the greater the influence you can exert. The makeup of magnet force-fields depicts this point.

A magnet exerts a force field that enables it to either attract or repel objects. The stronger this force-field is, the bigger the object it can attract or repel. One of the ways you can increase the force-field of a magnet is to attach it to a bigger magnet. The combination of the two force-fields then allows for the attraction of even bigger objects. Influence is like a force-field emanating from your life. The more influence your life is exposed to, the more of it you can exert.

The God-Influence

The ultimate source of irresistible influence is God. Aligning yourself to the God-influence makes you influential on the earth. The Bible uses several synonymous terms such as the "blessing of God", "anointing of God", "favor of God", "grace of God", "Spirit of God", "the presence of God" and "the power of God" to refer to the influence of God on a person.

These terms all speak of the operation of God within and upon a person that enables him or her to function with increased abilities, results and impact in the affairs of life. These terms speak of God alighting on imperfect human flesh and then doing what only He can do. Meditate on the following passages of scriptures.

"The Lord was with Joseph, and he was a successful man; and he was in the house of his master the Egyptian. And his master saw that the Lord was with him and that the Lord made all he did to prosper in his hand. So Joseph found favor in his sight, and served him. Then he made him overseer of his house, and all that he had he put under his authority. So it was, from the time that he had made him overseer of his house and all that he had, that the Lord blessed the Egyptian's house for Joseph's sake; and the blessing of the Lord was on all that he had in the house and in the field" (Genesis 39:2-5).

"And God gave Solomon wisdom and exceedingly great understanding, and largeness of heart like the sand on the seashore. Thus Solomon's wisdom excelled the wisdom of all the men of the East and all the wisdom of Egypt. For he was wiser than all men— than Ethan the Ezrahite, and

Heman, Chalcol, and Darda, the sons of Mahol; and his fame was in all the surrounding nations...And men of all nations, from all the kings of the earth who had heard of his wisdom, came to hear the wisdom of Solomon"
(1 Kings 4:29-31, 34).

John came baptizing in the wilderness and preaching a baptism of repentance for the remission of sins. Then all the land of Judea, and those from Jerusalem, went out to him and were all baptized by him in the Jordan River, confessing their sins" (Mark 1:4, 5).

"Then Jesus returned in the power of the Spirit to Galilee, and news of Him went out through all the surrounding region. And He taught in their synagogues, being glorified by all. So He came to Nazareth, where He had been brought up. And as His custom was, He went into the synagogue on the Sabbath day, and stood up to read. And He was handed the book of the prophet Isaiah. And when He had opened the book, He found the place where it was written: "The Spirit of the Lord is upon Me, Because He has anointed Me to preach the gospel to the poor; He has

sent Me to heal the brokenhearted, to proclaim liberty to the captives And recovery of sight to the blind, to set at liberty those who are oppressed; to proclaim the acceptable year of the Lord" (Luke 4:14-18).

"And through the hands of the apostles many signs and wonders were done among the people. And they were all with one accord in Solomon's Porch. Yet none of the rest dared join them, but the people esteemed them highly. And believers were increasingly added to the Lord, multitudes of both men and women, so that they brought the sick out into the streets and laid them on beds and couches, that at least the shadow of Peter passing by might fall on some of them. Also a multitude gathered from the surrounding cities to Jerusalem, bringing sick people and those who were tormented by unclean spirits, and they were all healed" (Acts 5:12-16).

"Then news of these things came to the ears of the church in Jerusalem, and they sent out Barnabas to go as far as Antioch. When he came and had seen the grace of God, he was glad, and encouraged them all that with purpose of

heart they should continue with the Lord. For he was a good man, full of the Holy Spirit and of faith. And a great many people were added to the Lord" (Acts 11:22-24).

These are just a few examples of how the touch of God upon people in the form of wisdom, power and grace produced influence that motivated, attracted, and impacted people and places. All these instances have something in common. The main actors retained influence after an initial encounter with God by remaining under God's influence, much like the moon remains in the path of the sun's rays.

How to Increase God's Influence in your Life

You must have your own encounter with God that changes the trajectory of your life. It begins with the surrender of your life to Christ as Lord and continues as you walk in faith with Him. These encounters do not have to be dramatic. Praise God if they are! But, God also works in simple supernatural ways to transform our lives as we walk with Him. You can help in this effort. By actively seeking these encounters, you increase the likelihood of their occurrence and are better prepared when they do occur. The following are some practical steps you can take to increase the influence of God in your life. These steps will work for anyone who consistently practices them. It does not matter where you are in your faith walk right now. If you follow these steps, they will increase God's influence in your life.

1. Passionate Pursuit

Desperation and pursuit are major qualifications for promotion in the kingdom of God. It is those that are poor in spirit, those that hunger and thirst, that will be blessed (Matthew 5:3, 6). Hungry and desperate people always catch Jesus' attention.

For example, the woman with the issue of blood defied laws banning her from appearing publicly and pressed through a crowd just to touch the hem of Jesus' garment. Her efforts granted her the healing she so desperately sought. Likewise, the paralyzed man whose friends broke the roof in order to get him closer to Jesus also received an audience with Christ. Blind Bartimaeus screamed loudly, tearing off his beggar's garb as he ran to Jesus. He certainly got Jesus' attention. Zacchaeus got Jesus' attention by climbing a tree. These people flaunted social convention, risking embarrassment and ostracism in their zeal to encounter God.

In the Old Testament, Jacob displays a similar thirst. Jacob resorted to deception to get his brother, Esau's blessing. Esau, on the other hand, because he had little value for his blessing, lost it. God honored Jacob's desperation. God allowed the blessing to be transferred to Jacob despite his wrongful actions. God focused instead on the thirst for God which motivated Jacob's actions.

You must also become so desperate for the presence and influence of God upon your life, that you go the extra mile to secure its manifestation in your life. You will need to plan for it and expect it. Do not wait for it to accidentally drop on your life but, proactively pursue it. Plan for it in your schedule. Seek counsel on what you can do to secure it, then execute you plans. Spiritual hunger displayed shows the level of value. God will honor your value of His influence demonstrated by your pursuit.

2. Being with Him

A few years ago, I had to regularly visit the home of an individual I was discipling. He was a new believer who still battled a smoking habit. Many times when I would leave his house after the personal bible study I was conducting with him, I would have the smell of cigarette smoke all over me.

Though he did not smoke in my presence, the residue of the smoke in his house got on my clothes. Anyone who met me after I left his house would have concluded that I was a smoker. As a result of spending so much time with a smoker, unknowingly, what was on him and around him got on me and I reeked of cigarette smoke.

Our associations work in a similar way. As you spend time with people, there is a transfer, or impartation, that occurs. There is an impartation of wisdom, foolishness, mannerisms, faith, fear, attitude, and more as you spend time with people. I will dwell more on impartation as it relates to people in the next chapter but for now the focus is God.

Acts 4:13 says:

"Now when they saw the boldness of Peter and John, and perceived that they were uneducated and untrained men, they marveled. And they realized that they had been with Jesus."

Peter and John were uneducated, but through their association with Jesus over the past three years, something from Him had rubbed on them. Everyone could see it. Peter and John discussed the scriptures with the authority of educated people. They were displaying the same boldness and power for which Jesus was known. By spending time with Jesus, they had received transference of His influence.

Like the disciples, Moses also received an impartation after spending time in the presence of God. Moses spent forty days on Mount Sinai with God. By the time Moses left the presence of God, his face was shining with God's glory. Moses was reflecting the light and glory that the King of Glory and the Light of the World had radiated upon him. The glory and light transferred to Moses was so much that the no one could look directly at his face. Moses had to cover his face with a veil.

God is the influencer extraordinaire! You cannot meet with Him and remain the same. As you fellowship with Him you will be transformed. Once you begin to walk with Him, your mediocrity goes. If your life remains untransformed, it means you are not living in His presence. You have not had an encounter with Him. The book of John says it this way,

Under The Influence

"This is the message which we have heard from Him and declare to you, that God is light and in Him is no darkness at all. If we say that we have fellowship with Him, and walk in darkness, we lie and do not practice the truth. But if we walk in the light as He is in the light, we have fellowship with one another, and the blood of Jesus Christ His Son cleanses us from all sin" (1 John 1:5-7).

Follow your hunger for Him with daily communion with Him. Every time you appear in His presence, an aspect of His nature rubs off on you. You catch His compassion, love, wisdom and grace. You begin to wear His fragrance and smell like Him. If you stay in His presence, people will start noticing His influence on your life. Your words will start to carry His power. Your atmosphere becomes charged with His presence.

For example, Peter spent so much time in God's presence that people were healed even when only his shadow passed over them. Paul wrote,

> *"But we all, with unveiled face, beholding as in a mirror the glory of the Lord, are being transformed into the same image from glory to glory, just as by the Spirit of the Lord"* (2 Corinthians 3:18).

The more time we spend with Him, the more like Him we become. Like the moon, we start to reflect His glory and influence in our sphere.

3. Meditating on the Word

Another practice that can increase God's influence in your life is meditation. The words of God are conveyors of His influence. As you interact with them and make them the focus of your thoughts, they begin to influence your life. Psalm 1:1-3 celebrates the influence of God on a person who gives priority to God's word.

> *"Blessed is the man who walks not in the counsel of the ungodly, nor stands in the path of sinners, nor sits in the seat of the scornful; but his delight is in the law of the Lord, and in His law he meditates day and night. He shall be like a tree planted by the rivers of water, that brings*

forth its fruit in its season, whose leaf also shall not wither; and whatever he does shall prosper."

Psalm 112:1-4 has a similar message,

"Praise the Lord! Blessed is the man who fears the Lord, who delights greatly in His commandments. His descendants will be mighty on earth; the generation of the upright will be blessed. Wealth and riches will be in his house, and his righteousness endures forever. Unto the upright there arises light in the darkness; He is gracious, and full of compassion, and righteous."

Meditating on the word of God renews your mind and grants you access to the necessary ingredients of great influence.

4. A Lifestyle of Praise and Worship

Praise unleashes the presence and the influence of God upon a life or an atmosphere. This is because God lives inside of His praise.

IRRESISTIBLE INFLUENCE

"But You are holy, Enthroned in the praises of Israel" (Psalm 22:3).

As you praise Him, His presence increases tangibly around you and begins to influence your environment. He is a jealous God, so other influences vying for control will fall, much like statues of Dagon, the Philistine God, fell down and was broken once the ark of God was brought into the Philistine temple. God's influence extends into and takes over atmospheres in which He is praised. Live a lifestyle of praise and worship and your life will be blessed with an increase of influence.

CHAPTER 4

Associating With Influence

"Show me your friend and I'll tell you who you are"

- Author Unknown

In the last chapter, we focused on increasing your influence through your walk with God. We saw that correct positioning in fellowship with God increases influence. Now, we extend the same principle to human relationships. You can increase your influence by carefully choosing the types of people you associate with.

Five Effects of Association

1. Your association will directly influence your character and attitude

"He who walks with wise men will be wise, but the companion of fools will be destroyed." (Proverbs 13:20).

Just as you can increase your influence through fellowship with God, you can also increase your influence by carefully choosing the types of people with whom you associate. You actually become like those with whom you associate.

As you interact closely with people, you increasingly become more like them. This is the law of association: there is an exchange and transfer of attitudes and characteristics by people who spend enough time together. Paul attests to this idea by writing,

"Do not be deceived: "Evil company corrupts good habits" " (1 Corinthians 15:33).

The old saying goes, "show me your friend and I'll tell you who you are". You are going to average out the characteristics of the people you associate with. This is the reason why good parents carefully monitor the types of friends their children keep and the places they frequent. They know that given time, they would take on the characters of their friends.

2. Your association affects your environment

People have certain auras—particular atmospheres surrounding them. When you associate with them closely for long enough, you share the same atmosphere. The spiritual and emotional environment around them diffuses into yours.

Have you noticed that your encounters with some individuals leave you sad, angry or frustrated? You felt differently before your contact with them; but, after your time with them, you sensed a totally different atmosphere around you. Your calm may have been disturbed. You may become more susceptible to temptations. You may have felt depressed. What happened is that they just transferred the aura around their lives to yours.

Conversely, there are other people who leave you inspired, joyful, and full of faith and hope. They leave you refreshed. These people have the right kind of atmosphere surrounding them. They are the kinds of people with whom you should spend most of your time. Developing close relationships with them will allow you to consistently cloak yourself in their positive atmosphere. Saul met the prophets and he also began to prophecy (1 Samuel 10:11). The atmosphere of the prophets got on him. Do the people you move with have such positive effects on you?

3. Association will either increase, diminish or multiply the God-influence on you

In addition to affecting your atmosphere, your associations affect the level of the God-influence flowing in your life. They will either block or enhance the flow. In his book, "Winning with People" John Maxwell wrote about four kinds of people that will come into our lives.[4] The following is a brief description of them.

a. Adders: These are people who deposit good things into your life. They are good influences. They are usually good friends, confidants and godly family members. You will recognize them by what happens to you in their presence. When you are with them, you feel inspired, loved and believed in. They intentionally add value to your life and make your life more pleasant and enjoyable, thus increasing your capacity for influence. Celebrate this people.

b. Subtractors: This set of people take from you unintentionally. Being with them puts a burden on you. They drain you of energy. They are receivers not givers. You will recognize them by your response when they initiate contact with you. They are those you hesitate to pick up their phone calls. Tolerate these people.

c. Multipliers: These are people who multiply your life. They greatly enhance you. They push you to be better. These are usually mentors and leaders. They push you into your potential. They are your coaches and not necessarily your friends. They will not tolerate your weaknesses; but will confront them. They love you and seek your increase. They multiply influence in your life.

Value these people. Never take them for granted. Appreciate and celebrate them.

d. Dividers: These are people who cause strife and greatly diminish your life. They are different from subtractors because they are intentionally causing harm. You should avoid such people.

You need to identify those who occupy these categories in your life. Your response to each group should be different. Spend most of your time with adders and multipliers. Sometimes it may require some sacrifice to get to be with them. Pay the price. Sometimes your association with multipliers will be through their materials such as books and videos. Immerse yourself in them. The more you spend time with them, the sharper you become.

> *"As iron sharpens iron, so a man sharpens the countenance of his friend" (Proverbs 27:17).*

Your cutting edge in life becomes more effective as you associate with adders and multipliers.

On the other hand, try to limit your interaction with subtractors and dividers. Tolerate the subtractors but if possible, avoid the dividers. It is also important that you do not become a subtractor or divider. Work to be a multiplier or adder to other people. Seek to give in relationships not simply to get.

4. Association will either limit or enlarge your vision

The following story illustrates the power associations can have to limit potentials. There was an eaglet that fell from the safety of its nest while it was young. A farmer found the young eaglet and took it to his farm. He raised the eaglet in a chicken coop among his many chickens.

As the eagle grew up, it began to act like the chickens around it. It ate what the chickens ate and pretty much did everything the chickens did. Though it was a very powerful eagle that could soar in the sky, it was grounded and did not fly.

IRRESISTIBLE INFLUENCE

One day, a man came to the farm and saw the eagle acting like a chicken. He immediately recognized the problem. The man decided to help this eagle discover itself. He separated it from the chickens and took it to a very tall part of the farmhouse, but the eagle still could not fly.

Later the man took the eagle far away to a high mountain where they could no longer see the farm house. Other eagles soared in the mountain. The man released the eagle and soon it was flapping its wing and flying.

As long as they were close to the chicken coop, the eagle could not fly. It took a dramatic change of company from chickens to fellow eagles before the eagle could unleash its potential.

Change Your Company

Like this eaglet, you may need to change your company if the law of impartation is working against you. If you are surrounded by chickens, there are two

Associating With Influence

things that have to change. You have to leave the coop *and* you have to leave the company of chickens. You were created to fly in unrestricted skies.

Lot, Abraham's nephew's life also demonstrates how associations can limit your potential. When God told Abraham to leave his father's house to a land God would show him, without any instruction from God, Lot attached himself to Abraham and left with him. Lot soon began to enjoy the same blessings that Abraham received. Lot became very wealthy as a result of his association with Abraham.

Later, he made a mistake and separated from Abraham. When Lot moved close to Sodom and Gomorrah, he was exposed to the lifestyle of the land. This move almost cost him everything. Association matters.

5. Your association affects your reach

Frigyes Karinthy came up with the "Six Degrees of Separation" concept which proposes a human web in which each person is linked to any other person in the world by at most approximately six people. This idea speaks to reach, the number of people to whom you are connected. Influence works through reach. Association multiplies your reach.

As you associate, you jump from degree to degree towards people that need your influence. Every individual you see has a certain circle and will still expand that circle. Therefore, your association of influence with that individual will extend your influence beyond your own current circle with unlimited possibilities.

I have seen this concept at work in my life. As I develop relationships with certain individuals, suddenly, I find myself influencing their circles. I have seen families influenced through my association with just one member of the family. I have seen churches and other institutions influenced through my life as a result of my association with certain individuals who have access to those places.

Always be conscious of the fact that every individual you see has a certain circle and will still expand that circle. Your association of influence with that individual will extend your influence beyond your own current circle with unlimited possibilities.

Bill Bright's ministry, Campus Crusade for Christ also demonstrates this principle. This ministry was founded in 1951 at the University of California, Los Angeles in order to impact future leaders.

From their initial relationships with University of California college students, the organization's influence has grown to reach more than 190 countries around the world, employing over 25,000 full-time missionaries and has trained over 225,000 volunteers around the world. This ministries initial reach of college students extended through the ever growing associations of these students to reach its current network. This is an amazing example of multiplying influence into ever increasing circles by means of relationships.

The Power of Partnership

Another important way relationships multiply influence is through the power of partnership and collaboration. Ecclesiastes 4: 9 speaks about the power of partnership,

> *"Two are better than one, because they have a good reward for their labor"*

Two are better. To be better means to have good qualities to a greater degree than another. It means to be superior. Whatever is better is an enhanced and increased form of the other. So, two people are an enhancement of one. They operate on a greater degree than an individual.

Associating With Influence

Relationships multiply individual efforts. What you can do alone, you can multiply by joining with others. There is an enhancement of result and strength when individuals come together with one focus.

When the influence of God is upon the relationship, the principle of agreement applies. One of my favorite passages in scriptures, Deuteronomy 32:30 explains the principle of agreement. "How could one chase a thousand," the passage asks, "and two put ten thousand to flight, unless their Rock had sold them, and the Lord had surrendered them?"

I love the progression in the passage. It wasn't arithmetic but a geometric progression. If one chases a thousand, you would expect two to chase two thousand. But, rather, the passage says ten thousand. Because of God's involvement, the addition of one multiplied the result ten-fold.

This is the principle of agreement at work. Jesus seemed to utilize this principle when he sent out his disciples two by two to the cities in very successful missions. The early church followed a similar pattern, displaying various combinations of ministry partners such as Paul and Silas and Paul and Barnabas.

Geese flight patterns display the art of partnership with a slightly larger group. Geese fly using a "V" pattern which allows each goose in flight to have an equal field of vision. A goose leads the formation, doing most of the work. When the lead goose becomes tired, it moves to the back and another goose takes its place in front.

This rotation continues through their flight. As a result, the geese conserve energy. Another advantage of the V flight pattern is that as each goose flaps its wings, it creates additional uplift for the bird immediately following.

So, if one goose falls out of the formation, it immediately feels a drag or wind resistance that moves it to rejoin the group. Also, throughout the flight, geese at

Associating With Influence

the back honk to encourage the ones in front to keep the pace. Within this system, each goose's success is based squarely on the geese with which it has partnered.

As you make friends, be aware that your associations will influence you. Your ability to fly may be achieved or restricted through your associations. Have influence on your mind as you contemplate linking up and getting closer to people.

CHAPTER 5

Influential Prayer

"More things are wrought by prayer than these world dreams of" *- Alfred Tennyson*

I feel ashamed to say that there are some portions of the Bible with which I struggle. I do not have a problem believing them—I believe the whole Bible is the inerrant word of God. I struggle with these passages because I find them boring and wonder why God included them. I know all portions of scripture are inspired by God and are profitable, however, some portions—I'm talking about the genealogies—make me wonder.

You know the genealogies, right? They are the parts of the Bible in which verse after verse is a series of hard to pronounce names of people who lived for so and so years and then died—but, not before begetting people with equally difficult to pronounce names. The pattern continues for long periods until I find myself skipping over a few begats. Now, you tell me you've never done this before and we'll crown you the Bible Study King!

The first book of Chronicles is a paradise of begats. It contains nine chapters of genealogies. On one of those yearly read-through-the-entire-Bible exercises, I was about to do my usual speed reading, when 1 Chronicles 4:9-10 caught my attention.

"Now Jabez was more honorable than his brothers, and his mother called his name Jabez, saying, 'Because I bore him in pain.' And Jabez called on the Lord saying, 'Oh, that You would bless me indeed and enlarge my territory, that Your hand would be with me, and that You would keep me from evil, that I may not cause pain!' So God granted him what he requested."

Wow! This was a gem buried within a sea of begats. Hidden in my least favorite part of scriptures was a unique story of an outstanding man. According to the text, Jabez's birth was such an unpleasant experience for his mother that she gave him a name that meant 'he causes pain.' Imagine naming your child "pain in the neck." How do you think the child would feel once he understood the meaning of his name? Even if he did not care, with their ridicule, his classmates would have made sure he did.

A More Honorable Man

Jabez grew up under a name—a prophecy—of doom. For the first part of his life, under the prophecy of his name, Jabez was destined to cause pain. Jabez rebelled against this prophesy, choosing to reach to the Most High God who changes names and destinies.

How Jabez developed this faith is not told to us. Maybe he had heard about others like Abram and Jacob whose names were changed by God. Maybe, through his knowledge of these stories, he understood that God could overturn the destiny his name prophesied.

IRRESISTIBLE INFLUENCE

The Prayer of Jabez

So Jabez prayed. His prayer was essentially a cry to God for a release of the blessing upon him that would cause his influence to increase, while annulling his appointment with pain because of his accursed name. Jabez prayed for an enlargement of coast, an increase in his borders. He cried out to God to expand the circle of his influence. He wanted to go beyond his history, name and expected destiny.

He wanted God to give him a second lease at life. One characterized by usefulness, impact, and influence. He was not going to settle for mediocrity or limitations. He was not going to conform to the norms around him. He wasn't going to die as a footnote in history. He desperately wanted a different life than he he'd lived so far. He wanted his life to count. He took his desires to God in prayer and God granted him what he requested.

Jabez' Biblical snippet ends there without telling us exactly how his coast was enlarged but I'm sure of this:

Influential Prayer

If he was a student, he must have ended up like a student in the order of Daniel, whose excellence made him an icon in Babylon and brought glory to God.

If he was a business man, his business would have expanded to serve multiplied customers and employed many beyond what he ever dreamed of.

If he was a minister, the impact of his ministry would have expanded to reach new people and places, beyond anything he had ever done.

We do not know. So I can only speculate. But whatever his calling was. As the blessing of God took over his life, his influence must have expanded supernaturally by the mighty hand of God that came on his life in answer to his request. A desperate prayer changed a man's destiny and expanded his influence.

I do know however, how the prayer of Jabez has changed *my* life. I first stumbled on this scripture during my college days. I determined that I would not just pass through my college but would leave an impact that would outlast my tenure. So, like Jabez, I began to pray daily for impact, influence and for the enlargement of my coast. God began to move and through the pastoral work I did then, many young people are still being thrust into God's purposes for their lives over a decade since I left the school.

The same hunger came on me when I left college. So, I sought God consistently for expanded influence for His glory in my pastorate in Lagos, Nigeria. God began to move as we pivoted to reaching the up and coming generation in colleges and high schools across our region. Years after I had moved on to my current location, those young ones we were reaching have gone on to establish more churches and initiatives for the kingdom of God.

I am currently pastoring the CityLight Church in Chicago and we're crying out to God with the same theme as Jabez. We are already seeing God move as a new company of people with a passion for the kingdom are being raised. We are trusting God for an increase in influence to make a name for Him in our city and nation.

You Too Can Pray

God does not show partiality. What he's done for others, He can do for you. It was God who inspired the human writers of the bible to pen the story of Jabez. In the mind of God, who perfectly inspired the scriptures, this story would one day give hope to someone who is in the same position as Jabez was. It would inspire a similar cry and invoke a similar answer.

If you are hungry for a life that makes a mark, if you are tired of living a limited, unfruitful life or, if you want to live a life of irresistible influence, then you need to start crying to God daily until you begin to have the borders of your life enlarged. Pray until your life becomes one of great impact in your generation. Speak to God about your increase until your life becomes a noteworthy one, not just one that is in the footnotes of history.

Prayer Influence

Though there's a specific power in the prayer of Jabez, prayer in general is important because it has the power to influence. Praying is one of the most influential things you could ever do. Prayer gives you access to the ears of the judge of the universe, the King of kings and the Lord of lords. It gives you the privilege to move the very hand that moves the universe. Physical boundaries and logical limitations do not restrict prayer.

For instance, you may not have physical access to the White House, but through prayer, you can exert influence there. Likewise, you may not be able to enter nations closed to the influence of the gospel, but, through prayers your influence can penetrate the bamboo and iron curtains of the world. Through prayer, you can follow missionaries into unreached regions of the earth without stepping a foot out of your bedroom.

Influential Prayer

You can touch the raunchiest bar or brothel in your community and push away the influence of darkness. You can reach war-torn nations, bringing hope to millions of hungry children. You can influence the laws and decisions of public officials in your community and nation. You can stand in the gap and turn away the wrath of God, securing His mercy.

Use this privilege. Prayer is not the exclusive preserve of a few great saints. Also, it is not just for those who can spend countless hours in prayer, but also for those whose schedules limit them to just minutes per day. It is not the volume of prayer that matters, but the focus, fervency and persistence.

Your level or station in life does not exclude you from the privilege of prayer. Nursing mothers can pray and exert influence, busy professionals can do it. Salespeople can do it as they go about their calls. Incarcerated ones can engage in it. God will hear your cries if you seek Him. He will take your every request according to His will and use it as a tool to extend His kingdom and establish His purpose on the earth. *"Before you call, God will answer. While you are speaking, He will hear."* (Isaiah 65:24). From you, words of prayers will proceed that will extend God's influence beyond your borders. You will be a useful vessel in the hand of God.

Pray for Your Loved Ones

"Isaac prayed to the Lord on behalf of his wife, because she was childless. The Lord answered his prayer, and his wife Rebekah became pregnant" (Genesis 25:21).

Isaac and Rebekah faced a situation that could have brought confusion and despair. Isaac chose to address this situation by turning to God in prayer. God answered him and gave them twin children who were potential nations. Out of the barren situation, nations were born. Prayer is powerful. There is no greater way to exercise influence over the circumstances and situations you or your loved ones face than through prayer.

You will also be confronted with other difficult situations regarding your loved ones. Other issues like a loved one struggling with depression, a spouse who can't seem to keep his job, an addicted family member, a friend with a struggling business, a sick relative, a wayward child, or a child struggling at school may arise. And, these are just a few examples. The good news is that no matter what the situation is, you can do exactly what Isaac did. You can pray to God on behalf of your loved ones and expect Him to answer.

The author, Stormie Omartian has sold more than twelve million copies of her books. Her body of work includes, The Power of a Praying Wife, The Power of a Praying Parent, The Power of a Praying Husband, The Power of a Praying Woman, and The Power of Praying Together. In all her books, she speaks about the power of prayer to change people and situations with an emphasis on the family.

Her books emphasize that a praying wife can invoke the power of God to change her husband for good and the husband can do likewise. People who have used her prayer guidelines have testimonies about positive changes in the lives of those for whom they prayed. Those stories are proofs of the efficacy of prayers for loved ones.

The answer to your prayers may not come packaged exactly as you expect or manifest immediately. But, if you leave the situation in God's hands and continue to pray and praise Him in spite of the situation, doing whatever He directs you to do about it; you will definitely see God intervening in the situation.

This is because God honors the persistent prayers of His children, especially as they pray for others. Throughout Jesus' ministry, people brought their loved ones' issues to Jesus. Friends brought their paralyzed buddy to Him. Mothers and fathers brought sick children. A master brought a sick servant. Peter's

Influential Prayer

mother-in-law was healed. Jesus demonstrated over and over in all these situations that God honors the faith of his children on behalf of their loved ones.

Jonathan Edwards, the famous Great Awakening preacher best known for the sermon, *"Sinners in the Hand of an Angry God"* got married to his wife Sara in 1727. The Edwards had 11 kids. Every night Jonathan Edwards was home, he would sit for one hour with his kids talking with them and praying over them. In 1900, 400 descendants of the Edwards were tracked down.

Here's what was discovered: 285 of them were college graduates, 300 were preachers, 13 were acclaimed authors, 13 college presidents, 65 professors, 100 lawyers, 1 dean of a law school, 30 judges, 56 doctors, 1 dean of a medical school 80 office holders, 3 U.S senators, 1 Vice President of the U.S and 1 Comptroller for the U.S Treasury.

Because of the obedience of the Edwards in living for God and in praying for their children, blessings extended to generations after them and to people unknown to them that their descendants had served in all these positions. You can affect your progeny in a similar way. Pray often for your children. Saturate their lives with God's influence. Your prayers will be seeds that will influence their lives.

As well as praying for your children, praying for your community and the world in general is another important focus of intercessory prayer. Jeremiah 29:7 says,

"Seek the peace of the city where I have caused you to be carried away captive, and pray to the Lord for it; for in its peace you will have peace."

Throughout the years, various Christians have interceded with phenomenal results. For instance, God put a burden in the heart of John Knox, to pray constantly for his country. In his hideout, He would pray night after night, agonizingly crying "Lord, give me Scotland or I die!" His wife would beg him to get some sleep but he would tell her, ""How can I sleep when my land is not saved?" God gave him Scotland. Revival broke out. Multitudes were saved.

David Brainerd, missionary to the American Indians, felt a similar burden in his ministry. He described it in a diary entry he wrote on April 19, 1742,

"I set apart this day for fasting and prayer to prepare me for the ministry. In the forenoon, I felt a power of intercession for immortal souls. In the afternoon, God enabled me so to agonize in prayer that I was quite wet with sweat, though in the shade and the cool wind. My soul was drawn out very much for the world: I gasped for multitudes of souls. I think I had more enlargement for sinners than for the children of God, though I felt as if I could spend my life in cries for both.".[5]

A similar commitment was displayed by John Hyde, a missionary to India. Hyde was who was nicknamed Praying Hyde, after laboring for several years, with no fruit, would cry out over India before God,

" Father, give me these souls or I die!" by the end of his missionary work, he had won hundreds of souls into the kingdom.

All these individuals engaged in the prayer of intercession. Abraham gave us an example of this type of prayer when he prayed for Sodom.

"The men turned away and went toward Sodom, but Abraham remained standing before the Lord. What if there are fifty righteous people in the city? Will you really sweep it away and not spare the place for the sake of the fifty righteous people in it? Far be it from you to do such a thing—to kill the righteous with the wicked, treating the righteous and the wicked alike. Far be it from you! Will not the Judge of all the earth do right?" The Lord said, "If I find fifty righteous people in the city of Sodom, I will spare the whole place for their sake...Then he said, "May the Lord not be angry, but let me speak just once more. What if only ten can be found there?" He answered, "For the sake of ten, I will not destroy it" (Genesis 18:22-32).

Influential Prayer

Intercessory prayer is a type in which people, who have the privilege of being in relationship with God, leverage that privilege to secure God's mercy on behalf of those who are far from Him. It is praying for others in order to avert God's judgment on them. It is invoking God's mercy on behalf of those who have provoked His judgment by their sins. It is standing in the gap for people in prayer before God.

You can pray intercessory prayers for friends, families, strangers, communities and nations. Intercession is necessary because there are many individuals around us who have no relationship with God yet and are heading in the direction of God's judgment, knowingly or unknowingly.

These examples demonstrate the power of intercession. Intercession establishes the will of God in people's lives and communities. It links them with things that they cannot grasp by themselves. For example, praying for those who have not known the Lord prepares their hearts to receive the gospel and precipitates divine orchestrations of God to bring people across their paths with the gospel. Praying for neighbors opens them up to receiving the gospel. Praying for your community and nations establishes the will of God there. Praying for leaders surrounds them with the influence of God as they carry out their duties.

God is seeking intercessors. In fact, He puts people in locations, among certain types of people that need his mercy so that these intercessors could pray for them.

"I looked for someone among them who would build up the wall and stand before me in the gap on behalf of the land so I would not have to destroy it, but I found no one. So I will pour out my wrath on them and consume them with my fiery anger, bringing down on their own heads all they have done, declares the Sovereign Lord"
(Ezekiel 22: 30-31).

Influential Prayer

God's desire is for you to influence your community. Your presence there is strategic. You are put there by God to influence people with your interactions with them *and* your interaction with God. Look around you and identify the people He has surrounded you with in your family, neighborhood, workplace, school or nation. These people need God.

God put you there so you could start praying for them. Do not complain about your location, nation and family. Stop worrying about your children, fretting about the condition of your community or lamenting the problems in other nations. Begin to contend for them with God. Bring your supplications to God like Abraham did. God is merciful. He will hear and change their hearts and situations and draw them to himself.

I hope you are stirred up to pray and beyond that to actually schedule prayer into your daily activities. This is where influence begins. I pray that God will give you amazing encounters in prayer and make it one of the greatest adventures you will ever embark upon in life.

CHAPTER 6

What's Your Thing?

"You weren't an accident. You weren't mass produced. You aren't an assembly-line product. You were deliberately planned, specifically gifted, and lovingly positioned on the earth by the Master Craftsman."
— Max Lucado

I once took a marketing course. In one of the classes we discussed the concept of product differentiation. Differentiation is the act of highlighting the distinguishing characteristics of a company's product. Examples of companies utilizing a differentiation strategy include: Dr. Pepper, focusing on the difference in its soft drink's taste; FedEx, highlighting superior service; Wal-Mart, highlighting value and savings and Rolex, highlighting prestige.

These companies spend millions of dollars to differentiate themselves from other companies. They understand a basic truth that it is not your similarities that provide recognition, but your differences.

You should apply the concept of product differentiation to your life. When God made you, He made an original, not a copy. You have physical characteristics unique to you alone out of the more than six billion people on earth. For instance, your thumbprint is unique. Now, it is not only in physiological characteristics that you are unique. You also have spiritual and mental qualities that separate you from others.

Designed to Specification

"For we are His workmanship, created in Christ Jesus for good works, which God prepared beforehand that we should walk in them." (Ephesians 2:10).

This passage implies that when God was creating you in Christ, He had a plan in mind. He planned some unique things for you to do before you were born and packaged you uniquely to fulfill them. At our church, CityLight, we use the phrase "your thing" to express this unique plan for our lives. So it is common to hear one member ask the other, "What's your thing?"

This is an expression that dares the other to differentiate him or herself. In a world full of copycats and duplicates, many echoes but few voices, it is important for you to separate yourself from the pack and truly identify and celebrate the unique things that distinguish you from others.

To make impact, you must know who you are and what makes you unique. In order to learn who you are, you must consult your creator. So I ask you too, "What's your thing?"

Aspects of your Uniqueness

Let me take you through a few aspects of "your thing".

1. It's a God-pleasure thing

A main purpose for which we are here is to please God.

Revelation 4: 11b says:

"...Thou hast created all things, and for thy pleasure they are and were created"

The ultimate goal of your life is to give God pleasure. There is a unique stream of worship from your life that God wants to take delight in. It's "your thing" to worship God, to live a life that gives Him joy continually. Worship is not only about singing. Singing is only one of the ways to convey worship. True worship is a surrendered life. It is the continual out pour of your being to God daily by honoring His word.

God is your creator. He is your manufacturer and you are His product. Every manufacturer has a purpose in mind before He creates anything. God knows why you are here. As you spend time with Him in worship and prayer, He begins to open your eyes to see that purpose. He shares with you His unique assignment for your life. As you study His word, which is His owner's manual for your life, you will learn how you are supposed to function maximally in life. He will share His thoughts about your life with you. You will become more acquainted with Him and thus yourself and your reason for being here.

2. It is a Contribution thing

Paul, close to the conclusion of his earthly life, reflected,

"For I am already being poured out as a drink offering, and the time of my departure is at hand. I have fought the good fight, I have finished the race, I have kept the faith. Finally, there is laid up for me the crown of righteousness, which the Lord, the righteous Judge, will give to me on that Day, and not to me only but also to all who have loved His appearing" (2 Timothy 4:6-8).

Like Paul, you have a good fight to fight, a race to finish and a faith to keep. You have a unique fight for which God has given you unique weapons. There is a unique contribution you are called to make on the earth. There is something that you are to add to this world that wasn't there before your came. There is a particular problem you were designed to solve. There are people and places waiting for the solutions you have to offer.

This assignment is uniquely yours, preplanned before your arrival here on earth. You are supposed to pour out of the deposit of God in you until there is nothing left.

Dr. Myles Munroe said the wealthiest place on earth is neither the diamond mines of South Africa nor the oil fields of the Middle East, but the graveyard. Because there, many unfulfilled potentials, callings, visions and dreams lie. So he determined that he was going to die empty. He decided to utilize all his potential and take nothing to the grave.

I have made the same commitment too. I will touch everyone I am supposed to touch, plant every church I'm supposed to plant, write every book I am supposed to write. I will not hold back or hoard. I will make my unique contribution on the earth. Make this same commitment. Declare that you will not hold back or hoard anything God has invested in you.

3. It's a Sphere Thing

Make a commitment to discover into which spheres of life God wants you to pour your life. Your unique contribution in life will be through one or more of these spheres of influence. I use the letters A-G in remembering them.

A- Arts, Entertainment and Sports

B- Business and Finance

C- Church and Religion

D- Distribution and Media

E- Education, Science and Technology

F- Family and Home

G- Government and Law

Devote yourself to using your gifts to extend the influence of God on your life in that sphere. Reach people and reclaim that portion of the earth for the kingdom of God.

4. It's a SHAPE Thing

I came across the concept of the SHAPE, the unique design of everyone for the fulfillment of their assignments in life, in Rick Warren's *The Purpose Driven Life*. SHAPE is an acronym that stands for:

S - Spiritual gifts. When you became a believer, certain gifts begin to function in your life as a result of the workings of the Holy Spirit. Identifying these gifts can help you understand your place in life.

H - Heart. This has to do with your passion. Mike Murdock says, "The people that unlock your compassion are the ones you've been sent to". What you love is a pointer to what you are called to do. The problems that infuriate you are the one's you've been called to correct.

A - Abilities. These are natural talents and abilities that you possess like singing, writing etc.

P - Personality. Everyone is a combination of certain personality traits called temperaments. Some are introverts, others extroverts. God wants to express Himself through your unique personality. You don't have to become another person. You are the best you that He needs.

E - Experience. This includes family, educational and career experience. Knowing God never wastes a hurt, your painful experiences are also included.[6]

Finding your SHAPE is a great exercise in understanding your unique design for influence on the earth. Your effectiveness comes out when using your spiritual gifts and abilities where your passion is, through your unique personality, utilizing your experiences as tools.

5. It's a Company Thing

Another thing that differentiates you is the specific company of people with whom you are supposed to fulfill your life's purpose. Your calling will not be fulfilled in isolation but in a company—first within the context of the body of Christ as a whole and, then, specifically as part of a local expression of that universal body. There is a local church to which God has assigned you where you will best be able to grow and contribute to the increase of the body of Christ.

You will be unable to walk in the fullness of your calling if you hop from church to church or refuse to be part of a church. Joining a church on the internet or on TV is not enough. You must be physically part of a local church if you have the freedom in your nation to do so. Paul, in Ephesians emphasizes committed church membership as an essential part of spiritual growth.

What's Your Thing?

"But, speaking the truth in love, may grow up in all things into Him who is the head—Christ—from whom the whole body, joined and knit together by what every joint supplies, according to the effective working by which every part does its share, causes growth of the body for the edifying of itself in love" (Ephesians 4:15)

Ways in Which Church Membership Promotes Growth

A. Fellowship and Partnership: You are a member of the body. Every organ in a body needs other organs to survive and carry out its role. A church provides opportunities for fellowship with like-minded believers. You will have a pool of partners who you can join and support in the fulfillment of your callings. Your family will also have a place they can call their spiritual home and in which they can develop godly relationships.

"So now you Gentiles are no longer strangers and foreigners. You are citizens along with all of God's holy people. You are members of God's family" (Ephesians 2:19, NLT).

B. Support and Covering: Every calling of God will be opposed by Satan. So, in carrying out your assignment, you will face challenges, oppositions and tough situations. You will even be tempted to quit. It is during those times that your positioning in a church provides a covering for you.

As a member of a church, you will have people that pray for you, counsel you, stand with you and encourage you. You will have shepherds who watch over your life and feed you with knowledge and wisdom.

"And being let go, they went to their own companions and reported all that the chief priests and elders had said to them. So when they heard that, they raised their voice to God with one accord and said: "Lord, You are God, who made heaven and earth and the sea, and all that is in them"" (Acts 4:23,24).

C. Equipping: Being part of a local church also exposes you to the ministry gifts of the pastor, teacher, prophets, evangelists and apostles. These ministry offices were set in the church by Jesus, the head of the church for the purpose of equipping believers for the work of their ministry. In other words, they have been specifically gifted by God to help you find and fulfill your calling.

"And He Himself gave some to be apostles, some prophets, some evangelists, and some pastors and teachers, for the equipping of the saints for the work of ministry, for the edifying of the body of Christ" (Ephesians 4:11).

D. Corporate Anointing: Being part of a local church multiplies the anointing that is effectively working in your life. When believers fellowship together, each brings the specific anointing of God on them. Their anointing is combined, forming a more complete expression of God's grace. This is what is called the corporate anointing.

The corporate anointing is what happens when more than one believer is in the same place and there is a singleness of purpose between them. The Scriptures indicate that not only is this somewhat different from the individual anointing in the sense that it affects more than one person, but also that the corporate anointing seems to be one of greater power.

"When the Day of Pentecost had fully come, they were all with one accord in one place. And suddenly there came a sound from heaven, as of a rushing mighty wind, and it filled the whole house where they were sitting. Then there appeared to them divided tongues, as of fire, and one sat upon each of them. And they were all filled with the Holy Spirit and began to speak with other tongues, as the Spirit gave them utterance." (Acts 2:1-3).

Notice the words "all," "they," "them" and "each" in the passage. What they experienced here was both individual and corporate. Notice the same thing in the following passage:

"So when they heard that, they raised their voice to God with one accord and said: "Lord, You are God, who made heaven and earth and the sea, and all that is in them...And when they had prayed, the place where they were assembled together was shaken; and they were all

filled with the Holy Spirit, and they spoke the word of God with boldness" (Acts 4:24, 31).

E. A Launching Pad: A local church will also provide a launching pad for your calling. As you find a place of service within the local church, God begins to train you for greater use. Your faithfulness in serving at your local church prepares you for an ever expanding circle of influence. You can be commissioned into your unique calling and also have others join to assist and support you. This was what happened to Paul and Barnabas at the beginning of their missionary ministry.

"Now in the church that was at Antioch there were certain prophets and teachers: Barnabas, Simeon who was called Niger, Lucius of Cyrene, Manaen who had been brought up with Herod the tetrarch, and Saul. As they ministered to the Lord and fasted, the Holy Spirit said, "Now separate to Me Barnabas and Saul for the work to which I have called them." Then, having fasted and prayed, and laid hands on them, they sent them away. So, being sent out by the Holy Spirit, they went down to Seleucia, and from

there they sailed to Cyprus. And when they arrived in Salamis, they preached the word of God in the synagogues of the Jews. They also had John as their assistant "
(Acts 13:1-5).

Equipped with these passages, find your company. Locate a Bible believing and practicing church. Stay planted there. If your present church does not provide these opportunities, change churches. All that you need for influence will flow from the root of your church into your life.

"Those who are planted in the house of the Lord shall flourish in the courts of our God. They shall still bear fruit in old age; they shall be fresh and flourishing"
(Psalm 92:13, 14).

6. It's a Value Thing

Another thing that differentiates you from others is your values. Your values are the highest priorities of your life. They are the unique set of governing principles to each person's life. They are the fundamental building blocks of your personality. They are represented by the clearest answer you can give to these questions: What is non-negotiable in my life? What are the most important things in my life?

Alternatively, imagine that you died and by some means you are an invisible guest at your funeral. Your family and friends are gathered to talk about your life. What would you want them to say about you? The answer to these questions also represents your values.

To differentiate yourself for influence, you should identify these values. You can accomplish this by writing down your values. I did this exercise and came up with the following set of values:

1. I love the Lord with all my heart, mind and strength

2. I am an outstanding husband and father

3. I honor my father and mother and love my family

4. I manage my life's assets e.g. health, time, possessions excellently

5. I am involved in constant and never ending self-improvement

6. I am a good and dependable friend, loving and kind to everyone in my network of relationships

7. I am an excellent pastor and church leader

8. I am a good citizen who cares about the plight of people in my nation

9. I am using all my God-given creativity to make new things to solve problems in the world

10. I witness the gospel regularly and disciple people and raise leaders.

These represent things that are the highest priorities in my life. I admonish you to do the same. Grab a pen. Do it now. Don't procrastinate. We are never perfect in performing these values. There is always a gap between our values and our present realities. But, as we improve, we experience peace, something Abraham

Maslow called Self-actualization—the bringing together of what I do and what I really value.

A Personal Constitution

At the CityLight Church, I teach people involved in our leadership training – the Leading Lights; to put all these dimensions of their uniqueness into a document we call a personal constitution. The purpose of this document is to act as a reminder of the unique things about their lives that differentiate them from others. This document also highlights the attributes through which these leaders could extend the influence of the kingdom of God. You might find it useful to create your own Constitution.

The kingdom of God is expanded and your life becomes fulfilling as you tap into your uniqueness, investing it in others and in the mission of the kingdom. The light in you must not be hidden. No man lights a lamp and puts it under a table. It is time to shine your light, to be an influence in your world by discovering your purpose, sphere, shape, church and life values.

CHAPTER 7

The Salt Factor

"You can impress people from a distance, but only impact them up close" – John Maxwell

When I got saved, I would often wonder why Christ did not just return immediately and rescue believers from this corrupt world. Why let us continue going through the trouble of living in a decaying world, having to struggle with the devil, the world and even our flesh?

Why couldn't He just make it a rule that once someone surrenders to Him, the person undergoes a personal rapture, gets take away from this world of sin to be with the Master immediately?

It wasn't until I began to study on the purpose of God for our lives and his plans on the earth that I understood why things are the way they are. The following verse of scriptures was one of the answers to my question. The message translation reads:

"Let me tell you why you are here. You're here to be salt-seasoning that brings out the God-flavors of this earth. If you lose your saltiness, how will people taste godliness? You've lost your usefulness and will end up in the garbage" (Matt 5:13, MSG).

Jesus had the ability to say many things in a few words using parables. This little parable contains a lot of information. It reveals one of the main reasons why we are still in the world. Like salt in a soup, we were left here to be influencers on the earth, to keep it from growing totally rotten until the time appointed by God for the return of Christ. I call this the salt factor. Let's dig a little deeper into this parable.

The Nature of Salt

Getting born again is a total nature change. It is not a just a conversion or acceptance into a church. It is the birth of a new creation in Christ (2 Corinthians 5:17). When people get born again, they become the salt of the earth. It means you are wired for influence. There is something in your makeup that has the capability of affecting your environment and changing it. This is your salt nature.

The Capacity of Salt

What can this nature do?

1. Salt seasons. Salt adds flavor to the soup. Without salt, the soup is bland and tasteless. Similarly, your presence in your family, community or nation is supposed to add flavor to the place. Things should get better because of your presence. Life should taste sweeter for someone because of your presence.

2. Salt preserves. Salt protects from decay and decomposition. It stops meat from rotting. You are a preserving factor wherever you are located. For example, you are to be an intercessor for the people in the places where God has put you. God arranges for believers to be in certain locations, at certain times, among certain types of people that need his mercy so that they can pray for them. Again, as we have seen, He said,

> *"So I sought for a man among them who would make a wall, and stand in the gap before Me on behalf of the land, that I should not destroy it; but I found no one. Therefore I have poured out My indignation on them; I have consumed them with the fire of My wrath; and I have recompensed their deeds on their own heads," says the Lord God" (Ezekiel 22: 30-31).*

Be aware of your preserving ability and privilege and use it.

3. Salt hurts. When salt is applied to a wound, it stings. In the same way, don't expect that everything God leads you to say or do is going to be loved and received well by those to whom you are sent, even though your intentions are good. You want to bring healing, but people might take it wrongly. In fact, there are certain people in the world right now who are great influences for God but are hated by the masses. They are hated because they speak the bitter truth. Their saltiness hurts some people. It might well be that those who rise up and oppose you are experiencing a sting from the salt you are applying to their wounds, so don't stop.

4. Salt cleanses. Being salt, your influence ought to bring some cleansing to the places you go. I remember a time I used to visit the home of one of the people I was discipling for a weekly bible study.

Before we started having the bible in the house, the place was a gathering spot for various unsaved people. Men and women met at the place and had sexual intercourse, watching obscene programs on TV.

However, after we started the bible study, many of those people either stayed away or joined us in the bible study. Soon, what was being watched on TV changed. The presence of believers in the house forced a cleansing.

5. Salt creates thirst. Salt also creates a thirst. This is an expression of the salt influence to create a cry in the heart of people it touches for water. Your influence can make people want more of God. You can create a longing in the hearts of those you influence for the same kind of relationship you have with God. For unbelievers who never realized their need for God or even believers that have let the cares of this world distract them from their first love.

Salt Principles

Salt alone can make no difference except certain things are in place. The following describes some important principles of influence from the characteristics of salt.

1. Influence Comes Through Proximity and Reach.

Salt cannot do its work unless it is in contact with what it is meant to salt. It cannot work in isolation. You cannot make a difference and impart your salt flavor if you do not make contact with the people and places that need to be flavored. This was the error of the church in recent times. Because of the misinterpretation of the biblical teaching of separation from the world, believers withdrew completely from all the venues of influencing the culture of the society. We withdrew and huddled together in our churches waiting for Jesus to appear and rescue us from the world of sin.

The result was that the world became more sinful because of the absence of enough Christian witness. Now when we send our kids to school or turn on the TV, it is with trepidation because we do not know what may follow. This was not the method of Jesus. He was holy but he interacted with publicans and sinners. He ate and drank with them.

The same dynamic occurred in the urban cities of America. The decaying inner cities of today were once homes for people, many of them believers, who could have acted as salt in those neighborhoods to prevent them from decay, but once the neighborhoods began to change, those people all fled to the suburbs, allowing decay to take its toll. Thank God, a reverse trend is beginning to occur as urban mission-minded believers are being called of God to relocate back into those communities to bring empowerment and hope.

The Christian Community Development Association of which I am a member, started by Dr. John Perkins recognizes the importance of the salt factor. That is why the first principle in Perkin's philosophy of Christian community development is relocation. Relocation involves moving into the neighborhood you desire to have influence in just as Jesus relocated from heaven in order to save us.

> "The Word became flesh and dwelt among us, and we beheld His glory as of the only begotten from the Father, full of grace and truth" (John 1:14).

Jesus relocated. He didn't commute back and forth between heaven and earth. Similarly, if you want to be an effective influence of the gospel, you will have to incarnationally go among those you wish to reach. Influence works through reach and contact. We must engage the systems of this world, learn how they operate and deliberately infiltrate them with kingdom-minded believers who will bring their unique God-flavors into them. We are not to be afraid of culture, isolating ourselves in our churches. We have to intentionally set out to transform the culture.

2. Influence Comes Through Identification. When salt comes in contact with the soup, it dissolves. It becomes invisible and begins to look like the soup in which it is immersed. This important characteristic of salt speaks to how you must approach influence.

Not only do you have you make contact through incarnation, you must fully identify with what you want to influence. Paul was referring to this principle of identification when he said,

"For though I am free from all men, I have made myself a servant to all, that I might win the more; and to the Jews I

became as a Jew, that I might win Jews; to those who are under the law, as under the law, that I might win those who are under the law; to those who are without law, as without law (not being without law toward God, but under law toward Christ), that I might win those who are without law; to the weak I became as weak, that I might win the weak. I have become all things to all men, that I might by all means save some" (1 Corinthians 9:19-22).

Paul identified with those he desired to influence. You have to do the same. If you want to be an influence in the business arena, you must learn about business and walk with business people. You should be able to speak the language of business people. If you want to influence youths in the family sphere, you will need to learn their language, love them enough to be with them and identify with them.

3. Influence Grows by Spreading. When salt comes in contact with the soup, it spreads throughout the soup. If it does not spread, some parts of the soup will be saltier while the other parts will fail to experience the savor even though salt is present. This is another important principle of influence. To maximize influence, seek to spread out to everywhere possible, not just to certain parts.

Think of how the church has concentrated in the church and religious sphere while the other six spheres of influence: business, media, education, family and government have been almost neglected. The church sphere is over-salted while the other spheres barely have a Christian presence.

If you are a pastor, seek to spread your messages and disciples to all the spheres. If you are a writer, seek every avenue of getting your book out. Use every available voice. When new technologies emerge, do not shy away from them or treat them with suspicion. Doing this creates a vacuum that ungodly influences will gladly fill.

I still know of some pastors who discourage their members from joining Twitter or Facebook because they might be wrongly influenced. I know there are cases of church members who have rekindled old flames through these social media and have gotten into sin. So definitely, some need to stay out if it is a source of temptation to them.

However, it should not be a rule for all believers. We need many believers in these media arena to be the salt there. Otherwise, these arenas would be completely taken over by the enemy.

4. Transformation. Salt transforms the soup. This is the goal of kingdom influence; to change lives, places and things. Your influence should never be for the sake of influence alone, but should be aimed at bringing transformation. You want to make the kingdom atmosphere and systems the new prevailing order where darkness had ruled before. You want to bring healing, reformation and a turn-around to the order of things. This is the purpose of influence.

Your Response

Knowing the great prospect your life can be as the salt of the earth, there are two things you need to do. The first is to get out of the saltshaker and begin to make impact using the salt principles we just examined. Second you need to keep your saltiness like Jesus admonished.

Use these four principles to get out of the salt-shaker and plunge yourself into your place of influence. Be aware that there are many types of salt-shakers that restrict us from being salt to the earth. Fear, slothfulness and neglect all keep us trapped in salt-shakers. The holder of the shaker could even be a pastor.

Pastor Sunday Adelaja has a saying that some churches are like prisons, the members are the prisoners and the pastors are the wardens. Some pastors, because of insecurities hold down their members, refusing to empower or release them to fulfill their individual callings in life. If you are in such a church, you need to find another one. You need a place where you are trained as a kingdom arrow to be shot into a sphere of influence in the world.

How to Season your World

To conclude this chapter, I will like to put some feet to our discussion by suggesting some practical avenues through which you can fulfill your role as the salt of the earth.

1. Use Networks and Relationships

The first avenue of influence is through your network of relationships. This includes your family, work, business, church and other social networks. Start with the circles you already are in.

Apply the proximity principle: initiate deliberate contact with them through phone, email, face-to-face meeting or any other means in order to get closer to them. Think about ways you can represent Christ before them. Think of how they can get to experience God's character being displayed through your life and observe your practice of kingdom principles. Share your testimony with them. Tell them about Christ.

2. Be an Example in Excellence

The second way to season your world is to be an example of excellence. Strive for excellence in all you do, be it at home, work or school. Let your success be a challenge to those around you, and then let them know your source is Christ.

Let people see the conduct and outcomes of your service to Christ. Be a polished arrow in God's hand. Sharpen your skills, seeking more training and higher education if need be. Daniel became an influence in Babylon through his excellent spirit.

3. Season Through Compassion

Your compassionate help to the poor and the needy is a form of seasoning. Make use of opportunities that arise to help the needy. Every touch of help you give applies your salt into their lives. "Pure and genuine religion in the sight of God the Father means caring for orphans and widows in their distress." (James 1:27). Think of someone like Mother Teresa. She applied her salt seasoning to the world through her compassionate work among the poor.

4. Engage in Your Market-place Ministry

Another way to practically season your world is by engaging in your market-place ministry. This means you touch people and influence things right there in the place where you already spend the most of your time, at work. Jesus had 132 public appearances in the gospels. 122 were in the marketplace while 10 were in the synagogue.

Most of the miracles that were done by Jesus were in the public places. Out of the forty miracles documented in the book of Acts, only one was in church. Following the example of Jesus, you can also use your platform in the marketplace to shape the systems and influence people.

5. Package Your Gift Excellently

Your talents and gifts are tools for influence as we have seen earlier. They however need to be packaged so that they can reach more people and places. If your talent is writing, you can start by setting up a blog online, or writing a book. If it is singing, record your songs and put them out to bless others. The better packaged your gifts, the farther they can reach.

CHAPTER 8

Leading Influence

"Leadership is influence, nothing more, nothing less" –
John Maxwell

Influence is synonymous with leadership so I will not do justice to this study if we do not address the subject of leadership. The very definition of a leader is someone who exerts influence.

Dwight Eisenhower, the 34th president of the United States defined it by saying, "Leadership is the art of getting someone else to do something you want done because he wants to do it." Leadership is motivating people to move from one point to another.

Importance of Leadership

Leadership is essential. God uses leaders. If you trace the history of God's plans on the earth, you will see that God has always used leaders to carry out His plans. Starting from the very first chapter of Genesis, you see God creating the world and after making everything else, He forms Adam and gave him the assignment of ruling all of creation. God gave him the commission and the anointing to be a leader.

Think of all the great leaders of the bible – Moses, Joshua, David, Solomon, Peter, Paul, James and of course, the Lord Jesus. Five books of the bible were dedicated to the study of leaders and how they led, both good and bad. These are the books of Judges, I & II Kings and I & II Chronicles. In those books, God reveals the importance of good leaders and the detrimental effects of bad leaders regarding His plans on the earth.

One of my favorite leadership statements in the Bible is found in the book of Judges. The statement appears three times in the book.

Leading Influence

"In those days there was no king in Israel; everyone did what was right in his own eyes"
(Judges 17:6, 18:1, 21:25).

This passage shows that since there was no leadership, everyone did what they thought was right. You will see the disaster this led to as you read through the book. Notice also how God kept raising new leaders to move the people away from their sins and to lead them into victory against their enemies.

It is not only in biblical history that leadership has been essential. All through world history, we see great leaders who changed the course of history in various fields.

We know of military leaders who wrought great conquests to keep peace, preachers who brought reformation, statesmen who founded great nations and business leaders who spawned great enterprises. We have hundreds of biographies and autobiographies of these individuals. There are also those we often don't read of. Fathers who led their families well. Mothers – leaders themselves, who gave the world these great leaders.

Susanna Wesley comes to mind when I think of such unsung heroes of leadership. She was the wife of a poor and very difficult 18th century clergyman in a small parish. Though she had no formal education, she educated her 19 children.

Through her personal influence, she gave the world two great sons in the persons of Charles Wesley and John Wesley, the founders of the Methodist church and some of the greatest spiritual leaders the world has ever known. Because of her influence, it can be said that the Methodist movement began in the lap of Susanna Wesley.

God Still Needs Leaders

God still needs leaders who will cooperate with Him in carrying out His purpose on the earth. He wants leaders who will lead their families. He is searching for leaders who will pioneer causes dear to His heart in various locations around the globe. There is a constant desire in His heart for godly leaders in the nation and the community. Jesus spoke about that need in Matthew 9: 36-38,

"Then Jesus went about all the cities and villages, teaching in their synagogues, preaching the gospel of the kingdom, and healing every sickness and every disease among the people. But when He saw the multitudes, He was moved with compassion for them, because they were weary and scattered, like sheep having no shepherd. Then He said to His disciples, "The harvest truly is plentiful, but the laborers are few. Therefore pray the Lord of the harvest to send out laborers into His harvest.""

Shepherds are leaders. Jesus saw the need for leadership as He beheld the scattered multitudes. He saw the people scattered and harassed because they had no one to lead and tend to them. He instructed us to pray for leaders to be raised up who will labor in gathering in the lost sheep. Thus, Jesus identified the problem—a lack of leadership—and explained the first solution—prayer—in this passage. We need to pray today for strong leaders to be released in our homes, churches, communities and nations. We should pray for every sphere of influence in our nation to be filled with godly leaders raised and sent by God with unique assignments of influence.

We need more godly business leaders, more ministry gifts in the church sphere, more godly entertainers and media magnates. We need leaders in the family sphere. We should pray for God to thrust out more teachers and influencers in the educational sphere and of course godly leaders in the political and governmental arena.

We are also commanded to pray for current leaders. Paul wrote,

"Therefore I exhort first of all that supplications, prayers, intercessions, and giving of thanks be made for all men, for kings and all who are in authority, that we may lead a quiet and peaceable life in all godliness and reverence. For

this is good and acceptable in the sight of God our Savior, who desires all men to be saved and to come to the knowledge of the truth"
(I Timothy 2:1-4).

After identifying prayer as the first step, Jesus demonstrated the next steps that would need to occur.

"And when He had called His twelve disciples to Him, He gave them power over unclean spirits, to cast them out, and to heal all kinds of sickness and all kinds of disease...These twelve Jesus sent out..." (Matthew 10:1, 5).

Christ took personal initiative. He empowered and released the leaders under Him into the assignment. The task was huge. More leaders were needed, but He began with what He had. You can also do the same. You do not have to wait for others; you can take personal initiative and begin to develop and utilize your leadership skills no matter how inconsequential they may seem compared to the task at hand.

Everyone Can Be a Leader

Leaders are made not born. Though, some may be born with great propensity for leadership, their raw leadership talents have to be developed. Anyone can learn to be a leader, since we are all called to be influencers. In fact, everything we have talked about in this book is aimed at helping you become a better leader since leadership is influence.

This chapter is not a full treatise on leadership so we will not go too deep into the subject. My goal is to point you to what it takes to get on the path of becoming a better leader.

Steps to Leadership

1. Lead yourself.

Whenever the subject of leadership is discussed, we often think in terms of leading others. However, other people are not the greatest challenges we will face in leadership. We are going to be our own toughest leadership challenge. Self-leadership is the ability to influence and motivate yourself to be and do what it takes to accomplish God's goal for your life.

If you consistently apply the disciplines discussed in this book—such as displaying consistency in the spiritual discipline of prayer, remaining in God's presence, choosing your relationships, practicing integrity, and taking initiative—you will be leading yourself well.

Leading yourself also encompasses locating God's vision and purpose for your life. You can't lead if you are not going somewhere. People will follow you when they are certain you know where you are headed.

2. Become a Follower

If you want to be a great leader, you must first become a great follower. Remember what Jesus said to some of them when he called them, "Follow Me, and I will make you fishers of men." (Matthew 4:19). The greatest leaders in history began as successful followers.

Moses followed Jethro, his father-in-law. Joshua followed Moses. Elisha served Elijah for ten years before He got his mantle. The disciples followed Jesus followed for three years before they entered into the leadership of the church. Even the Lord followed. He first submitted to baptism by John the Baptist. Ultimately, He followed the Father to death on the cross.

Seeking to have authority without being under authority is an attempt to be in the place of God. This is what Lucifer did that led him to losing his place. God only must be the *Most* High. You can't. Having power without control is dangerous. Leaders who have never followed and are not following become tyrants. The ability to submit is an integral part of godly leadership.

Begin by following God, obeying His words and instructions for your life. Then, submit yourself to another leader: your pastor, boss or other godly leaders. It will be helpful if you follow someone in your sphere of influence. This person will model influence for you. Everyone needs a model. A model gives you a picture of what you can be and surpass. It gives you confidence that the level of influence you desire is achievable. If someone has gotten there, then you can also.

"We do not want you to become lazy but to imitate those who through faith and patience inherit what has been promised" (Hebrews 6:12).

3. Develop Your Leadership Skills

Your leadership skills can be developed by study and practice. Leadership has laws. Learn those laws through study. Dr. John Maxwell's book, *The 21 Irrefutable Laws of Leadership* is a very good book to utilize. Put what you learn into practice. Serve others. Touch hearts. Your leadership capacity will increase through practice.

4. Believe God for the Spirit of Leadership

"So Moses went out and told the people the words of the Lord, and he gathered the seventy men of the elders of the people and placed them around the tabernacle. Then the Lord came down in the cloud, and spoke to him, and took of the Spirit that was upon him, and placed the same upon the seventy elders; and it happened, when the Spirit rested upon them, that they prophesied, although they never did so again." (Numbers 11:24, 25).

Nothing God sends you to do is to be accomplished by your power. There is an anointing for each of God's assignments. There is a leadership anointing. Ask God for it. Get around those who have it and it will start rubbing on you.

If you will follow these steps, you will be well on your way to becoming a leader of influence for the Kingdom of God.

CHAPTER 9

Money and Influence

"There was a little city with few men in it; and a great king came against it, besieged it, and built great snares around it. Now there was found in it a poor wise man, and he by his wisdom delivered the city. Yet no one remembered that same poor man. Then I said: "Wisdom is better than strength. Nevertheless the poor man's wisdom is despised, and his words are not heard"
– King Solomon (Ecclesiastes 9:13-16).

The subject of money is one that evokes passionate reactions from people within and outside the church. My goal in this chapter is not to stoke those fires but to simply explain the connection between money and influence. My thesis is that money should be viewed as a tool for kingdom influence. That is what it is – a tool! It should not be seen differently from any other tool we use to propagate the gospel. Money is like the hammer we use to drive the nail of the gospel. It is like a saw we use to cut open hindrances to the propagation of the gospel. It definitely should not be loved, worshiped or overly emphasized.

Money is neutral. It is neither good nor bad. It takes on the morals of whoever has it. Likewise, being rich is a neutral. The things for which riches are used for determines the evil or good in the riches. There is no portion of the bible, which when properly interpreted, shows Gods condemnation of the possession of money.

When God expresses dissatisfaction in regards to riches, His displeasure is always aimed at the attitudes of humans not the money itself. Some examples of such scriptures are:

"Now godliness with contentment is great gain. For we brought nothing into this world, and it is certain we can carry nothing out. But those who desire to be rich fall into

temptation and a snare, and into many foolish and harmful lusts which drown men in destruction and perdition. For the love of money is a root of all kinds of evil, for which some have strayed from the faith in their greediness, and pierced themselves through with many sorrows" (1 Timothy 6: 6-10).

This passage is not a condemnation of being rich; the message of the passage is simply that money should never be our pursuit. It should not affect our emotions. True contentment and love do not come from money.

A second passage explains that we should not give money the affection of our heart.

"Do not lay up for yourselves treasures on earth, where moth and rust destroy and where thieves break in and steal; but lay up for yourselves treasures in heaven, where neither moth nor rust destroys and where thieves do not break in and steal. For where your treasure is, there your heart will be also...No one can serve two masters; for either he will hate the one and love the other, or else he

will be loyal to the one and despise the other. You cannot serve God and mammon" (Matthew 6: 19-24).

Paul says we should not trust in it or be moved by the abundance or the lack of it.

"Command those who are rich in this present age not to be haughty, nor to trust in uncertain riches but in the living God, who gives us richly all things to enjoy" (1 Timothy 6:17).

"Not that I speak in regard to need, for I have learned in whatever state I am, to be content: I know how to be abased, and I know how to abound. Everywhere and in all things I have learned both to be full and to be hungry, both to abound and to suffer need. I can do all things through Christ who strengthens me" (Philippians 4:11-13).

Money should never have our heart, affection, attention or trust. The presence or lack of it should never determine our joy or satisfaction. We should never worry about money or material possessions. Every time we allow money to dictate our emotions, we are giving it the place of God. God wants to occupy His place in our hearts. He wants to be the only one we expect to meet our needs.

Money Came Later

Pastor Sam Adeyemi tells a story from his ministry experience that demonstrates God's preeminence over money. At a point in Pastor Adeyemi's ministry, God began to inspire him to teach his members to start businesses. Some came to him, citing their lack of capital as the reason for their inability start. He took the issue to God.

While he was studying, God led him to Genesis 1 and asked him a question. "How much capital," God asked him, "did I have when I created the world?" Of course, the answer was none. God created the entire universe without a dime. Everything was made from intangibles. No dollar was expended. Pastor Adeyemi got the message.

God does not need money to meet your needs; that is why your affection should not be with money but with Him. Before money was invented, Adam and Eve had all their needs met in the garden.

This is what Jesus was getting at in Matthew 6:25-30,

"Therefore I say to you, do not worry about your life, what you will eat or what you will drink; nor about your body, what you will put on. Is not life more than food and the body more than clothing?
Look at the birds of the air, for they neither sow nor reap nor gather into barns; yet your heavenly Father feeds them. Are you not of more value than they? "So why do you worry about clothing? Consider the lilies of the field, how they grow: they neither toil nor spin; Now if God so clothes the grass of the field, which today is, and tomorrow

Money and Influence

is thrown into the oven, will He not much more clothe you, O you of little faith?"

Jesus demonstrated this fact many times. He multiplied bread when there was not enough money to purchase bread. When He needed to pay taxes, He simply sent Peter to look in a fish's mouth. He got a boat full of fish without spending a dime.

When He had no boat, He crossed the river by walking on water. When He needed a colt, He simply asked for it. When He needed the upper room to meet with His disciples, He demanded the room.

Money is an invention of man. So, the rules of money do not apply to God. God's supplies and provisions existed before money. Therefore, God should have your heart. The word of God is where your supply is located.

The Place of Money

Despite the fact that He did not need money, Jesus had a purse and a treasurer. He engaged in money transactions. Why would He use money, if He could operate without it? He used money because it is a medium of exchanging values on the earth. Money pays bills, taxes and school fees.

Church building contractors and employees will not accept a blessing alone as their compensation. The gas station will not accept a prayer, the laying on of hands and a positive confession in exchange of a full tank of gas. So, we must strike a balance.

Though money is not everything, money does do many things on earth. It is not all-powerful but it has power. It can buy food to feed the poor. It can buy books to educate poor kids. It can be used to buy airtime and internet access to beam the gospel through various media. Money can amplify the voices taking the gospel to the world.

Money and Influence

Though money could be doing this much good, the sad thing is that the prevalent influence of money in our world is evil. Money's influence is used to broadcast images that are destroying children around the world.

Money is used by corrupt politicians to buy the power to dominate us. Money is also used to run sex trafficking networks. In fact, one of the reasons people are willing to force fellow human beings into the sex trade is because of their corrupted allegiance to money.

The world's money is in the wrong hands. Money has suffered in the same manner that the spheres of the world have suffered from an absence of godly influence.

Through wrong teachings, the majority of the church has shied away from earning significant sums of money, teaching people instead that poverty is a virtue.

Some in the church, who have received God's revelation on finances, have been derailed off the middle of the road into unashamed materialism and selfish pursuits of money. We have to return to the truth of God's word to reclaim the influence. It is an urgent issue.

Money with a Mission

According to the scriptures, money has a part to play in the believer's commission. Money's purpose is defined in various parts of the bible.

1. To establish God's covenant,

Deuteronomy 8:18 says, "And you shall remember the Lord your God, for it is He who gives you power to get wealth, that He may establish His covenant which He swore to your fathers, as it is this day"
(Deuteronomy 8:18).

This verse makes it clear that God gives the power to get wealth. If wealth were evil, God would not give the power to get wealth to anyone. If He gave it to one generation, it means it is accessible to all generations but with conditions. One of the conditions is the purpose the wealth will be used for. This verse states that one of the purposes of this access is so that God can establish the covenant which He swore to Abraham, Isaac and Jacob.

What is this covenant He swore? Has it been established fully? A simple search through scriptures shows that the covenant is still pending full establishment since one of the promises of the covenant is that "all the nations of the earth will be blessed" through Abraham (Genesis 12:1-3). Paul then shows us in Galatians that the blessing referred to in Genesis is receiving the gospel of Jesus Christ,

> "And the Scripture, foreseeing that God would justify the Gentiles by faith, preached the gospel to Abraham beforehand, saying, "In you all the nations shall be blessed""" (Galatians 3:8).

This means the covenant is still being established through the preaching of the gospel. The Great Commission is the process through which God's covenant with Abraham to bless all nations is being established.

"Go therefore and make disciples of all the nations, baptizing them in the name of the Father and of the Son and of the Holy Spirit..." (Matthew 28:19).

This is the kingdom agenda, a task that requires the use of money. Lots of it! One of the missions of money is to send the gospel out to the ends of the earth, extending the influence of God's kingdom in hearts and places. Since it has not been fulfilled, we still have access to wealth as this verse promises.

2. Helping others – especially the poor.

Another purpose of money the scriptures spell out is the aid of the less fortunate. The following verses are self-explanatory.

Money and Influence

Proverbs 19:17 "He that hath pity upon the poor lendeth unto the LORD; and that which he hath given will he pay him again".

Acts 20:35 "I have shewed you all things, how that so labouring ye ought to support the weak, and to remember the words of the Lord Jesus, how he said, It is more blessed to give than to receive".

Romans 12:13 "Distributing to the necessity of saints; given to hospitality".

2 Corinthians 8:14 "But by an equality, [that] now at this time your abundance [may be a supply] for their want, that their abundance also may be [a supply] for your want: that there may be equality".

Ephesians 4:28 "Let him that stole steal no more: but rather let him labour, working with [his] hands the thing which is good, that he may have to give to him that needeth".

1 John 3:17 *"But whoso hath this world's good, and seeth his brother have need, and shutteth up his bowels [of compassion] from him, how dwelleth the love of God in him?"*

3. Extending Kingdom Influence

A third purpose for money is the extension of the Kingdom of God.

Recently I visited Luis Reyes, a pastor friend of mine in Zion, Illinois. During my visit to his church, he took me around his city to see the various kingdom projects in which his church was involved. We went from site to site. We saw a home for homeless teen boys his church just bought, one for homeless teen girls they were in the process of purchasing, a beautiful empowerment center to help small businesses, and an academic success center the church has just built.

While we were on our way, he said something that stuck with me. He said, "Satan has established his strongholds in our cities, we need to establish God's strongholds all over our cities too." A major way Satan has established his stronghold is by using money to establish his influence over our cities. The church has to wake up and start establishing God's strongholds all over the city too. This will require loads of finances to accomplish.

"Again proclaim, saying, 'Thus says the Lord of hosts: "My cities shall again spread out through prosperity; The Lord will again comfort Zion, And will again choose Jerusalem" (Zechariah 1:17).

If you have a vision of any kind, you will know the connection between money and vision. Without money, vision is grounded; it is like a car with no wheels. Churches cannot be built, tracts and bibles cannot be printed, and laborers in the gospel cannot be paid. This is not God's plan. His plan is for those who are on assignment for him to be amply funded. Paul said,

IRRESISTIBLE INFLUENCE

"Whoever goes to war at his own expense? Who plants a vineyard and does not eat of its fruit? Or who tends a flock and does not drink of the milk of the flock?" (1 Corinthians 9:7)

Satan fights this. His desire is to stop the church from having a voice. He wants to keep believers laboring under his system like Pharaoh wanted to keep Israel in Egypt under his bondage. He does not mind us going to church and worshiping as long as he has our substance under his control. He knows that if he holds on to our substance, we will eventually come back to him. We should respond to him like Moses did.

"Then Pharaoh called to Moses and said, "Go, serve the Lord; only let your flocks and your herds be kept back. Let your little ones also go with you"...Our livestock also shall go with us; not a hoof shall be left behind. For we must take some of them to serve the Lord our God, and even we do not know with what we must serve the Lord until we arrive there" (Exodus 10: 24, 26).

4. Honoring God

A fourth purpose for money is to honor God. Proverbs 3:9 says *"Honour the LORD with thy substance, and with the firstfruits of all thine increase"*. Money can be used to honor God. You can use it to honor His servants and bless His people. Paul rejoiced when the church in Philippi honored him with material resources, writing:

"Now you Philippians know also that in the beginning of the gospel, when I departed from Macedonia, no church shared with me concerning giving and receiving but you only. For even in Thessalonica you sent aid once and again for my necessities...Indeed I have all and abound. I am full, having received from Epaphroditus the things sent from you, a sweet-smelling aroma, an acceptable sacrifice, well pleasing to God. And my God shall supply all your need according to His riches in glory by Christ Jesus" (Philippians 4:15-19).

You must make impact and extend God's influence through your finances? Here is an action plan you can follow.

1. Break every emotional attachment to money and the mammon spirit. You do this by renewing your mind by meditating on the biblical purpose of money and the truth of God's sufficiency. Money is not your answer to any situation; God is. He can choose to use or not use money. Renew your mind to this truth, meditating until God becomes the only one you trust as your source.

2. Be Industrious. Work hard. Anyone that promises you riches without work is deceiving you. Get-rich-quick schemes are deceptions. They violate the seed principle of God's kingdom. It is the hand of the diligent that produces abundance. Your diligence is the channel that God uses to bless you.

3. Practice Generosity. Be generous to your family. Tithe to your church. Give to the needy. Make sure that material blessings proceed from your life to help others in need. Give to fellow Christians in need.

4. Practice good financial management. Use a budget. Eliminate wasteful spending. Save and invest out of your income. Prepare for the future.

5. Believe God. In all these, put your trust in God. You will need to demonstrate faith in God to receive His supplies.

Follow this plan and you will be in a position to exert irresistible influence through your finances to the glory of God.

CHAPTER 10

Let Your Light Shine

We are told to let our light shine, and if it does, we won't need to tell anybody it does. Lighthouses don't fire cannons to call attention to their shining- they just shine. - Dwight L. Moody

During a class on world religions I participated in while studying at Moody Bible Institute, one of the requirements was that every student had to visit at least three religious establishments different from a church in order to observe the religions and interact with the people as Christians with the aim of learning the best ways to evangelize to them. We were sort of like spies of the land.

I went with a friend of mine to visit a Hindu temple and a Buddhist temple. During the visits, I noticed a similar trend. We would sit at the back, quietly observing as the worshipers performed their rites. Throughout the services, members glanced at us. After their services were over, they came over, engaging us in conversation. Once we told them we were Christians an opportunity to share our faith was created.

After the visit to the Hindu temple, seeing the opportunity our simple presence created to share our faith in a place where darkness ruled, I thought of the following verse of Scripture. I like The Message translation of the verse.

"Here's another way to put it: You're here to be light, bringing out the God-colors in the world. God is not a secret to be kept. We're going public with this, as public as a city on a hill. If I make you light-bearers, you don't think I'm going to hide you under a bucket, do you? I'm putting you on a light stand. Now that I've put you there on a hilltop, on a light stand—shine! Keep open house; be generous with your lives. By opening up to others, you'll prompt people to open up with God, this generous Father in heaven." (Matthew 5:13-16)

Jesus called us the light of the world. We are to illuminate places of darkness. Think of how simple it is for light to penetrate darkness. It doesn't have to talk, fuss or strategize. It only has to be present and consistently turned on. Light only needs to be present for darkness to dissolve! Our presence in those temples was like lights turned on in the midst of darkness and it brought a little bit of illumination.

Light, at its core, is like influence. Let's look at some characteristics of light.

1. Light has a Source

Just like the source of your light is God, the source of your influence is also God. He is the true light that illuminates all. When you shine, you are simply reflecting God's marvelous light. In order to continue shining with growing intensity, you must stay positioned under His influence through prayer and obedience to His word.

2. Light must be turned on.

It is not enough to be connected to the source of power, light must be turned on in order for it to illuminate or influence. You also must be turned on. You turn on your light by living a life of faith and holiness in which you give glory to God for the blessing on your life.

You turn it on by knowing who you are in Christ and living it out. Whenever you practice any portion of scripture, you are turning your light on. Similarly, as you get involved in good works, showing compassion, people can see your light is turned on.

3. Light must be positioned.

You cannot have influence if you hide. Jesus said the purpose of light is not to be hidden but to be positioned in such a way that it illuminates. In the same way, you have to be positioned in places where your influence is relevant, sometimes this will be a place where darkness has prevailed. You may have to relocate, or step into situations where darkness is having a field day. For example, you may need to write a letter to the editor of your community newspaper to correct an erroneous article that denigrates Christ. Or, you might have to get a job in a workplace where darkness has ruled in order to bring some illumination there.

Believers are often nervous about inserting themselves into places where darkness thrives because they are afraid of contamination. However, light doesn't have to be afraid of darkness. You shouldn't have any problems if you put other things we have discussed in this book—such as being under a church covering, having a solid prayer life, living under the influence of God and keeping the right associations—in place.

So, boldly position yourself where your gifts can make a difference. Develop relationships with people your life can influence.

4. Light doesn't have to speak, it eliminates darkness by presence.

Sometimes all you need to do is to be present. Without a word spoken, your lifestyle can influence and make a difference. There is power in example. Paul, writing to his protégé, Timothy, instructs him on the power of living an exemplary life.

"Let no one despise your youth, but be an example to the believers in word, in conduct, in love, in spirit, in faith, in purity." (1 Timothy 4:12)

If Timothy followed Paul's instructions, he would exert and maintain Godly influence. Communicating a similar sentiment, Ralph Waldo Emerson once said "what you do speaks so loudly that I cannot hear what you say." A quote attributed to Francis of Assisi makes the point this way, "Preach the Gospel always, and if necessary, use words." These two quotes allude to the power of an exemplary lifestyle in exerting influence. How you live may be more influential than what you say.

"Do all things without complaining and disputing, that you may become blameless and harmless, children of God without fault in the midst of a crooked and perverse generation, among whom you shine as lights in the world, holding fast the word of life, so that I may rejoice in the day of Christ that I have not run in vain or labored in vain."(Philippians 2:14-16)

5. Light works with other lights.

Light does not compete with light. Instead, light simply joins together and brightens the room. Your influence increases as you link up with other people with influence. Look at a city street. The more street lights there are, the brighter the street. Likewise, it will take all the lights working together to bring illumination to the darkness of our cities and nation.

"But you are a chosen generation, a royal priesthood, a holy nation, His own special people, that you may

proclaim the praises of Him who called you out of darkness into His marvelous light;"

(1 Peter 2:9)

6. Light is not always received

"Jesus said, "And this is the condemnation, that the light has come into the world, and men loved darkness rather than light, because their deeds were evil. For everyone practicing evil hates the light and does not come to the light, lest his deeds should be exposed. But he who does the truth comes to the light, that his deeds may be clearly seen, that they have been done in God." (John 3:19-21)

As this passage explains, your attempt to illuminate and influence will not always be received well. Becoming a person of irresistible influence comes with a price. Not everyone will be happy with your vision. Great dreams when shared with others elicit a cross-section of responses. Adopters buy into it with excitement. Laggards watch to see what will happen to it. The indifferent couldn't care less about it. Opponents plot against it.

It is great when others like you and buy into your vision. However, the fact is that every time you attempt to carry out God's vision for your life, there will be some who feels threatened by it. There will be those who will hate you and your vision out of envy or jealousy. It shouldn't be surprising that these people may not be strangers; opposition to your vision will often rise from those closest to you. A man's enemy often is someone from his household.

Parents may think you are stupid. Siblings may think you are crazy. Your spouse may remind you of current commitments. Friends may ask you to be more reasonable. Your church may think you are misguided and proud. You need to understand that eyes can be blinded to light. Satan often interferes, causing people to doubt and oppose your efforts though they are good and may even be for their benefit. Paul was aware of this dynamic. He said,

IRRESISTIBLE INFLUENCE

"But even if our gospel is veiled, it is veiled to those who are perishing, whose minds the god of this age has blinded, who do not believe, lest the light of the gospel of the glory of Christ, who is the image of God, should shine on them."
(2 Corinthians 4:3, 4)

We see this blindness in the Bible. For instance, Joseph's family members felt threatened by Joseph's vision of influence. They thought he was proud. Likewise, the family of Jesus labeled him crazy. Paul was deemed mad from his abundant knowledge.

Your life may mirror that of many of these Biblical figures. Opposition will rise to your God-given vision from quarters that will surprise you. Those you thought had your back may stab you there. You will see blank stares of people as they mull your audacity to challenge the norm.

People will call you in for advising sessions, trying to talk you out of your vision. When these begin to happen, don't be surprised or discouraged. Your vision of influence is going through the normal process all great visions must go through. A vision unopposed is worth nothing. If you have no head-on collision with Satan, the opposition of the brethren, it means you are headed in the same direction. He knows that opposition from strangers is not as powerful as those from trusted ones.

Refuse to be moved. Stick with your vision. Analysis is good as long as it doesn't lead to paralysis. The sincere ones will eventually come around when your vision starts to bear fruit.

You may lose them for now, but it is only temporary if you stick with your vision. If you cave in, you may gain their approval now only to lose later because you missed the boat of God's call on your life and you are stuck in mediocrity with no influence.

I challenge to turn on your light and start shining. Begin your adventure into irresistible influence. God will be glorified, Christ will be exalted, people will be blessed, your community will be thankful and you will be fulfilled.

Meet the Greatest Person Alive!

I want to share with you about the most important decision that you can ever make in life. Jesus came to the earth to live and die, so that you might have life and live life abundantly, but the devil also has come to steal, kill and destroy. Winning or losing in life depends on whose lordship you are under; either Jesus or the devil. Romans 10:9 says that if you confess Jesus as Lord with your mouth and believe in your heart that God raised Him from the dead, you will be saved. You can yield your life over to the Lord Jesus Christ by saying this simple prayer:

Lord Jesus, I acknowledge that I'm a sinner. I believe that you came to the earth to die for my sins and you rose from the dead to give me life abundantly. I confess you as Lord of my life. I ask you to come into my heart and make me a brand new person. Amen.

If you just prayed this prayer and you meant it, Jesus has come into your life and has made you a brand new person. He has delivered you from the authority of the devil, and has given you dynamic power to live life abundantly. We will like to know of your decision, so that we can stand with you in prayer, and send you faith-building materials to help you in your walk with God.

Please write us at info@thecitylight.org or call our number toll-free: 1-888-LIGHT-21.

Bibliography

1. "influence." Merriam-Webster.com. 2011. http://www.merriam-webster.com (10 May 2011).

2. The Barna Group : *Most Twentysomethings Put Christianity on the Shelf Following Spiritually Active Teen Year.* http://www.barna.org (9 September 2011)

3. Jon Meacham, "The End of Christian America," Newsweek, 3 April 2009.

4. John C. Maxwell, Winning With People: Discover the People Principles that Work for You Every Time (Nashville: Thomas Nelson, 1996).

5. Jonathan Edwards, Life And Diary Of David Brainerd (New York: Cosimo, Inc., 2007).

6. Rick Warren, The Purpose Driven Life: What on Earth Am I Here For? (Pennsylvania: Running Press, 2003).

To order more copies of this book or other inspiring books visit:

www.thecitylight.org

www.pastorlan.com

More Books by the Author

Just Before You Say I Do: A Roadmap for Singles

Mission Possible

The Five Tests of Faith

Identity in Christ

The 31 Immutable Laws of Relationships

The CityLight Publications Vision

Proclaiming and spreading

The life-changing truth of the Gospel

Through Spirit-inspired literature;

Introducing Jesus to a needy world,

Bringing life-changing revelations to Christians;

Empowering them to live their best lives now.

www.ingramcontent.com/pod-product-compliance
Lightning Source LLC
Chambersburg PA
CBHW071503040426
42444CB00008B/1475